BUDDHA

ALSO BY NIKOS KAZANTZAKIS

Fiction
Zorba the Greek (1953)
The Greek Passion (1954)
Freedom or Death (1956)
The Last Temptation of Christ (1960)
Saint Francis (1962)
The Rock Garden (1963)
Toda Raba (1964)
The Fraticides (1964)

Poetry
The Odyssey: A Modern Sequel (1958)

Philosophy
The Saviors of God — Spiritual Exercises (1960)

Nonfiction
Japan-China (1963)
Spain (1963)
Journey to the Morea (1965)
Report to Greco (1965)
England (1966)

BUDDHA

Nikos Kazantzakis

Translated from the Greek by
Kimon Friar and Athena Dallas-Damis

AVANT
BOOKS

Published in 1983 by Avant Books
3719 Sixth Avenue
San Diego, California 92103

Library of Congress Catalog Card Number 81-71164.

Library of Congress Cataloging in Publication Data

Kazantzakis, Nikos, 1883-1957.
   Buddha.

   Translation of: Voudas.
   I. Title.
PA5610.K39V613 1983   889'.232   83-2642
ISBN 0-932238-18-1 (hardcover)
ISBN 0-932238-14-9 (paperback)

First Printing
Manufactured in the United States of America

CONTENTS

ABOUT THE TRANSLATORS

Kimon Friar was born of Greek parentage on an island on the Sea of Marmara, was brought to the United States at an early age, and returned to Greece in 1946. He has taught at the universities of Iowa, Adelphi, New York, Minnesota, Illinois, Indiana, California, and Amherst College.

His translations from the Greek include *The Odyssey: A Modern Sequel* (Simon & Shuster, 1958) and *The Saviors of God: Spiritual Exercises* (Simon & Shuster, 1961), both by Nikos Kazantzakis; *With Face to the Wall, Selected Poems of Miltos Sahtouris*, (Charioteer Press, Washington, D.C.); *Introduction to the Poetry of Odysseus Elytis* (Kedros, Athens, 1978); *The Sovereign Sun* (Temple University Press, 1974); *The Spiritual Odyssey of Nikos Kazantzakis: A Talk* (North Central Publishing Company, 1979); *The Stone Eyes of Medusa*, essays, (Kedros, Athens, 1981) in Greek.

Mr. Friar has directed The Poetry Center in New York for five years. His radio program on literature has been broadcast in New York, Chicago, and over The Voice of America in Greek. He is presently Greek Editor of *The Charioteer*, Greek associate of *Paideuma, A Journal of Ezra Pound Scholarship*, and Book Review Director of *The Athenian*.

For the quality of his translations and his contributions to modern Greek letters, Kimon Friar has received numerous honors and awards, among these the Greek World Award, 1978; a Ford Foundation Grant, 1975-77; and The Ingram Merrill Foundation Award, 1981-83.

Athena Dallas-Damis, is the translator of Nikos Kazantzakis' last novel *The Fratricides* (Simon and Shuster, 1964), his *Three Plays — Columbus, Kouros, Melissa* (Simon & Shuster, 1969), and R. Mouzaki's *Greek Dances for Americans* (Doubleday, 1981).

She has written two historic novels: *Island of the Winds* (Caratzas Signet, 1976-78), and its sequel *Windswept* (NAL/Signet, 1981), to be followed by the last of her Island Trilogy which deals with Greece during the 1800's.

Ms. Damis is also a recognized journalist and lecturer on the Greek experience. She is the recipient of many awards including the *Greek World Magazine Award*, the *Haleen Rasheed Award for Distinguished Achievement in the World of Letters*, and the *AHEPA Fifth District Nikos Kazantzakis Award*, and is listed in the Contemporary Authors Encyclopedia.

PREFACE
Michael Tobias

The many legends surrounding the life of Buddha all converge upon a river.
Having slipped from his native Nepalese village in darkness, he rode his horse
Kantaka up to a river's far bank, stepped down, and for the following six
years he struggled. Seated under the Bo-tree, steadfast to penance and
contemplation, he endeavored to acquit this world of suffering, warding off
the daily temptations of Mara, prince of evil. In deepest meditation, sustained
only by an offering of rice-milk brought to him by the woman Sujātā, he
strode bravely into a great and universal awareness, an electrical fence of
revelation. The Four Noble Truths and Eightfold Path comprise his principal
message, one that was variously interpreted throughout Asia. Whatever its
vagaries of style and emphasis — from Sri Lanka to Japan — Buddhism
proposed three compelling and homogeneous assertions: gentle self-denial,
compassion for all living things, and an approach to nirvana — the Absolute
Void — involving the human acceptance of contradiction throughout Nature.

China's magical Yangtze River contains all of the elements of Buddhism, in its
geography, associations, and manifest dualism. Plunging off the Golden Sands
(Kinsha) of Tibet into deep limestone gorges, it sweeps up Central Asia's
mineral into the richest wet rice plantations on earth. Dropping into Kiangsi
Province, heading Northwest, the river charges the land with wealth, becomes
myth, before emptying tranquilly into the sea near Shanghai. Saints, poets,
pandas, even the celebrated Yeti have mingled in caves and bamboo glens
along the river's shores. The founder of Sōtō Zen, Dōgen, worshipped such a
river as the very embodiment of perfect reality, the true dharma of
Buddhahood. Similarly, Genkū, twelfth century founder of Japanese Pure
Land Buddhism, saw the rivers and mountains as Buddha's one and only
paradise on earth. Such smooth-flowing contemplations have entered the very
pre-cognition of Oriental religion and nature worship. But if the river was a
heaven, it could also become a hell. Since ancient times the zealous farmer has
exhausted the soil underfoot, thereby prompting rampant erosion and
devastating floods. Hundreds-of-thousands of lives have been lost to the
confluence. No mere folklore, such yin/yang dialectics came to shape Chinese
agricultural civilization. The course of the river was, like Buddha himself, the
basis for Chinese cosmography.

Greek sensibility had its own access to cosmic antipodes. The most important
oracle of primordial Hellas was Delphi, where opposing personalities, Apollo

and Dionysus, were triumphantly merged. But the Greek mind stopped short of exhorting the Void. This life was just too luscious, nude, sensual and honey-washed to forsake so easily. The ascetic East and god-tanned West had never been so perfectly integrated in a drama before the work of Nikos Kazantzakis. His intoxication with nature was world-roving, at times severe and abstinent, at other times all-giving, indulgent. While he was attracted to monks and solitaires, to Spartan discipline and lofty ordeals, his sense of balance stayed ultimately clear of them. Only Kazantzakis' unique orientation to tragedy and spirituality, could have conceived and forged the striking juxtaposition which occurs in his play *Buddha*. The Yangtze River is not just a vital ecosystem, a religion of form and lavish beauty, a link between mankind and God. The river *is* Buddha, and the final flood is Buddha's deliverance. There in the river of dignity, where chaos usurps calm, and calm beckons after chaos, is the life of the farmer, the sage, the grandchild. All ancestors cavort and multiply in the haven of white water against which no bulwark, no sandbag is sufficient. The only salvation is to yield, to be ravished, carried in the wild spray, reborn.

INTRODUCTION
Peter Bien

*"My method...does not involve a denial of
spirit and body, but rather aims at the conquest
of them through the prowess of spirit and body."*
— Nikos Kazantzakis[1]

I

In the spring of 1941, Kazantzakis embarked on one of his most ambitious
works, the play *Yangtze*, now known under the title *Buddha*. If we consider
the seven months from Mussolini's invasion of Greece on October 28, 1940
until the capture of Crete by the Germans at the end of May 1941, we see in
condensed form the whole of human existence as Kazantzakis had conceived it
previously and had expressed it in earlier works. We see in the successful
Greek defense against Mussolini the noble and quixotic effort of a nation to do
the impossible, and then we see in the German victory the inexorable power of
an overwhelming fate nullifying all the effort that had preceded. Once more in
Buddha, as he had in the *Odyssey*, Kazantzakis set himself the task of
examining this totality of experience which seemed now to have been
confirmed in the political cataclysm he had just witnessed. The play is huge; it
presents not only the total situation but also various reactions to it, all of
which were facets of Kazantzakis's own conflicting reactions to the actual
events of 1940-1941. Specifically, it presents the reactions of a man torn
between the need to remain Buddhistically aloof from events and the opposite
need to participate in the world's ephemeral shadow-dance — to indulge in the
supreme folly of trying to act as though the phenomenal world were real. But
these contrary reactions are unified by the magic of the poetic imagination.
We may think back to a statement made by Kazantzakis in 1935:

> *I felt a great joy trying again to harmonize...fearful
> antitheses....Woe to him who sees only the mask! Woe to him
> who sees only what is hidden behind the mask! The perfect sight
> is to see simultaneously...the sweet mask and behind it the
> abominable face.*[2]

This statement provides as good a formulation as any of the essential material
of Kazantzakis's play, which shows imagination (perfect sight) comprehending
and reconciling the sweet mask of political action with the abominable face of
Buddhistic resignation.

Before examining *Yangtze* further, I would like to explore the problem of dating. We have four versions, three of which reached at least a completed draft. The first, written in Vienna in 1922, reflects Kazantzakis's extreme disillusion with politics as the result of the murder of Ion Dragoumis in 1920, the fall of Venizelos in the same year, and the abrupt end of Kazantzakis's own possibilities for action in Greece. The second, begun later in 1922, in Berlin, following the Asia Minor Disaster (September 1922) and Kazantzakis's meeting with a circle of communist Jewesses, reflects his growing ferocity, and his determination to act in some way, if not in Greece then in Russia. The third, planned during the period 1928-1932 but never executed, reflects Kazantzakis's disillusion with Soviet communism and with political activism. The fourth, which is the version we now possess, reflects, as I have suggested, the Albanian campaign against Mussolini and the subsequent defeat of Greece by Germany.

Let us survey the four versions in greater detail. The one begun in July 1922, in Vienna, was a tragedy in free verse. In *Report to Greco*, Kazantzakis describes his sojourn in Vienna at length, including how he contracted the hideous "ascetics' disease" as a result of his immersion in the Buddhistic vision. In a colloquy reported by a friend, he adds:

> I went to Vienna, where...I studied Buddhism with that chronic
> curiosity I had in my youth. I saw that there [in Buddhism] was to
> be found the vision of life toward which Nietzsche had been
> pushing me, and I became Buddha's disciple.

When Kazantzakis departed for Vienna three weeks after the elections that ended the Venizelist regime, he entered a lull between two periods of political activism: the Greek nationalism of 1919 and the communism that was to begin in Berlin in September 1922. Since he felt that the vanity of all effort had just been confirmed, he was ripe for a religious system which explained his sense of futility. At the same time, he was troubled by his continued attraction to literature. The relation of all this to the play is indicated in a letter:

> Whatever literature I write strikes me as an act of cowardice...,
> because I am afraid to confront the One: the only One who
> shouts inside me.... Individuality is worthless. But there used to
> be something else inside me, something higher than the wretched
> ego, something broader than myself....Alas, if only I could
> formulate these thoughts in "Buddha"! I'm telling myself that this
> work shall be art's last temptation for me....

Here, undisguised, is the agonizing so characteristic of Kazantzakis throughout his life. The attractions of beauty and metaphysics are clear from the passage, the attraction of politics just as clear from the context. His reaction here is also very characteristic: before giving himself over to political activity again, he must exorcise beauty and metaphysics by indulging them.

From the letter just cited, we might conclude that Kazantzakis was hoping simply to continue the free verse drama begun in Vienna. In the weeks that followed, however, he became more and more swept up in communist politics, and on October 15th he informed his wife Galatea, "I am rewriting *Buddha* in a new form — something fierce and bitter." Eventually, he reported that he had torn up the original version. The new effort was in highly stylized prose, presumably similar to that which he was to employ for the *Askitiki*[3] soon afterward. Subsequent passages in the letters confirm what we have already seen: his hope to exorcize the demon of art (beauty) and, through the play, to liberate himself for political action. When he finished the work he looked upon it as the beginning of a new phase in his development and said he wanted it "to become one of my major works."

We do not know how much of this second version survives in the final version. Probably very little. Near the end of his life, Kazantzakis told a friend that among the writings he had never published was one called *Buddha* in prose: "I tore it up."[4]

The third version occupied him off-and-on during the years 1930-1932, but never passed the planning stage. It is connected with his interest in the cinema, which he considered the perfect Buddhistic art form because of its "power to create people, ideas and passions out of light and shadow, and to annihilate them." "Oh, when will I begin *Buddha*, who is nothing but eye, who plays with the shadows, who knows that everything is an ephemeral creation of the ephemeral and complex human camera?" Obviously, we are moving in the direction of the play in its final form. This is seen even more clearly in a new prose work that Kazantzakis conceived in 1930. Provisionally named *En fumant*, this was meant to depict a period of reality encased between two dreams, the first involving art, the second metaphysics. He described it as "a work completely crazy, because I have in mind that it will never be printed. ...It will be the final form of *Buddha*." But external pressures never allowed him to go further with either project. Though he kept reading relevant books until 1932, he then began to speak of the work simply as "the future *Buddha*." Naturally, a theme that had meant so much to him over so long a period could not be forgotten. His chance came during the German occupation of Greece, which gave him an extended period of enforced solitude. In addition, the political events of 1940-1941 provided him with a renewed impetus to examine his conflicting needs (a) to remain aloof from events, and (b) to participate in the world's ephemeral shadow-dance. The subject of Buddha was a perfect one for a man who in the short span from October 28, 1940 to May 30, 1941 had seen enacted before his eyes the seemingly inevitable frustration of human hopes (the vanity of all desire central to Buddhistic teaching) and yet who, because of his renewed attachment to Greece, refused to accept the Buddhistic teaching easily and determined to indulge in the folly of trying to act as though the phenomenal world were real.

We know that *Yangtze* was begun during the terrible spring of 1941, with German planes flying overhead and strafing his neighbors. It was completed in first draft sometime before August 12th and then set aside while Kazantzakis turned his attention almost immediately to *Zorba the Greek* and afterwards to his translation of the *Iliad*. The second draft must have been composed between October 1942 and June 1943.

It is extremely important for anyone wishing to understand the final version to realize that it was written in this distressing period. On the other hand, it is equally important to remember that the call of Buddha to which Kazantzakis responded then (in the novel *Zorba* as well as in the play) is a call which he felt not only in 1941-1943, in a context of the Greek victory against Mussolini followed by defeat, but also in July 1922 in a context of disillusion with Greek nationalism, in October 1922 in a context of dedication to communist activism, and in 1928-1932 in a context of the extreme subjectivism that stemmed from his failure at direct action in the Soviet Union and manifested itself in his fascination with the cinema. At each stage we see a confirmation of Kazantzakis's ongoing need both to act in the world and to understand that such action is ultimately futile. In addition, in the third stage we encounter his discovery of a technique — reality encased in dream — by which he was finally able in the fourth and final stage of *Buddha* to create an appropriate form for this need of his to see simultaneously the sweet mask and behind it the abominable face.

II

We are now in a position to examine the play itself. The setting is China in the early twentieth century. As the curtain opens we view the central square of a village, with a huge statue of Buddha in the middle, the bamboo huts of the local whores on one side, the great gates of the palace on the other. The principal characters are Old Chiang, the war-lord; his son, Young Chiang; his daughter, Mei-Ling; and a Magician. Secondary characters are Young Chiang's wife, Li-Liang; the chief slave and his son; a Mandarin; Old Chiang's grandson; peasants, musicians, whores, and ancestors. Lastly, there are Buddha, his disciples, tempters, etc. The main plot is very simple. The Yangtze River is rising, threatening to flood the village and drown its inhabitants. The characters react to this threat in various ways that bring them into dramatic as well as philosophical conflict. As the curtain falls, the river is about to drown the entire cast (those who haven't already been killed or committed suicide) and presumably to wash away ancestors, bamboo huts, palace, and even Buddha. Except that the river *is* Buddha!

Added to this realistic part of the play, encasing it, is vision — art at the beginning, metaphysics at the end. In addition, the visionary element is inserted into each of the acts through the three pageants that are interwoven into the realistic action. These are the work of the Magician, who in turn is the functionary of the Poet who as Prologue makes us realize that everything we witness — Yangtze, suicides, passions, Buddha, heroism, resignation — is a plaything of the aesthetic imagination. All that we think is life, Kazantzakis is telling us, is a dream ending in nothing.

But the play's greatest surprise is that this seeming nihilism is not the last word. The last word is imagination, which explains why the author could insist in a gloss that his work, although it might seem pessimistic, is actually "a hymn to the pride and dignity of man." As for Kazantzakis's own career, this play is crucial because it is his first entirely open announcement of art as the ultimate salvation, subsuming activism (politics) and renunciation (Buddhism) without denigrating either. We remember Kazantzakis's yearning in 1922 to overcome his cowardice and to confront the One who was shouting inside him. Then, however, he still saw art as an impediment. Now, in the definitive version of the play, he speaks directly out of this Oneness in the person of the Poet who, by awakening imagination, makes possible the multiplicity that we call life. What Kazantzakis is attempting to say to us is that our normal concept of reality is outrageously incorrect, so incorrect that we come closer to truth with "play" than with seriousness. This is why he makes the Magician reject the commonsensical approach and instead play with the illusion of multiplicity, showing us the oneness behind youth, maturity and age, or behind life and death. He is the Artist and, as such, the source whence spring all the various characters, passions, births, deaths, hopes and fears of the deceptive multiplicity. This happens implicitly in every work of art, but Kazantzakis, by introducing the Magician and employing the frame technique, makes the artistic transformation explicit; although we react separately to the various actors and their problems, we also remain aware of the integral artistic energy behind them, an energy which stands as a positive value after everything else is annihilated.

When the Poet finishes his introduction and the "realistic" action finally begins (i.e. when the shadows commence to behave as though they were real), the subject matter is precisely the same as that already presented in the Poet's prologue and also in the Magician's preliminary instructions to a cast which projects the facets of his own oneness. This action is presented on two levels, on each of which we trace a kind of parabola meant to comprehend the totality of life and death. On the upper level, through the pageants, we see the life of Buddha. In the first pageant we have conjured up for us the attraction of women and earth, the temptations of activism, pride, anger, domestic concerns, patriotic duty — life's enticing multiplicity. In the second, we observe Buddha's spiritual exercises by which he overcomes the deceptive multiplicity of other egos and other civilizations, progressing toward the salvation of oneness. Finally, in the third pageant, Buddha debates with Wisdom and then with two ancient Greeks who speak movingly of "the power, the serenity, the nobility of the human species" and of mankind's willingness to fight for freedom. But for Buddha all this beauty and political struggle is a mask, a phantasmagoria of nothingness. Our salvation comes only after the cessation of desire and the welcoming of death as a release from life's torment. Thus at the end of the final pageant Buddha passes through the successive doorways of nonexistence until nothing remains except the song of the canary (imagination). In this, as in the previous two pageants, we are led from the unreal mask to the reality of nothingness as Buddha escapes the senses, conquers hope and fear, and finds in death the only consolation for pain, hate and blood. We mount the parabola of life and then descend again toward death. But Buddha is himself the sweet call of death; hence, paradoxically, Buddha is annihilated by Buddha. What we are meant to understand is that the two Buddhas, the one who strives and the one who negates, are the same.

The lower level is similar, except that lying in wait at the end of the parabolic journey is not Buddha this time but the Yangtze. Yet this difference is misleading. At the very end, as the river is about to wash away all the people, passions and buildings of the preceding "realistic" multiplicity, Old Chiang, guided by the Magician, realizes who the Yangtze really is. Crossing his arms and bowing to the rising river, he welcomes Buddha — and the lower level is united with the upper.

The journey from life to the acceptance of death, shown on the upper level through the history of Buddha, is shown on the lower through the minor characters and also through the two major ones. It is here, in this "realistic" part of the play, that Kazantzakis attempts to create the illusion that what the characters are struggling over is truly important. Said in another way, he attempts to convey the prowess of spirit and body that he had seen in real life ("real life"?) in 1940 and 1941 as he watched his nation confront first Mussolini and then Hitler. His challenge in this part is to keep Buddha from swallowing up life. Thus he gives us a "magic act" designed to cause us to mistake the puppets for living beings so that we, too, at least for a moment, may fall into the error of valuing the mask for its own sake. We should remember his admonition: "Woe to him who sees only what is hidden behind the mask…"

His technique on the lower level is to allow diverse personages to react in differing ways to the human condition. Let us consider the minor characters first. The whores persist in wanting flesh and kisses; they're not ready for salvation. The Mandarin places his hopes in history, thinking that he can anticipate disaster. But his "wisdom" is exposed as an inadequate defense against fate. Li-Liang, the wife of Young Chiang, has no independent being apart from her wifely role; therefore, when her husband falls victim to fate she commits suicide. The husband is very different. Europeanized, fiery, progressive, revolutionary and brutal, he is the antithesis of his father. He rebels against Buddha, ancestor worship and hashish smoking, replacing them with science, pragmatism and the cult of the future instead of the past. He wants to conquer slavery, injustice, hunger. He has the "divine sickness –– youth," which means that he wants to change the world overnight. His reaction to fate is a quixotic one: refusal to admit its existence. Yet, despite his youthful bravura, he is unable to make headway. His armies are defeated, his attempt at a palace coup fails, the dams he builds collapse and drown all the people he and his sister have indoctrinated in the new ways. In sum, he fails to conquer fate. Ironically, the great freedom-fighter ends as a kind of slave.

This is not true of the major characters, each of whom achieves freedom and salvation, but in a different manner. Mei-Ling, sister and accomplice of the revolutionary Young Chiang, is the opposite of the wifely Li-Liang; she is a "virgin lioness" who does not condescend to expend her energies upon husband, friend or son. Scorning small virtues, she knows that the ultimate virtue is to sacrifice herself futilely in a lost cause — futilely, that is, on the pragmatic level of results, tangible honor, and political efficacy. Though Mei-Ling throws herself into the river, no temple or plaque will be erected in her honor, the river will not be placated, the populace will not be saved — yet a "cry" will remain, affirming human solidarity and man's ability to confront fate with dignity. Like everyone else, Mei-Ling mounts one leg of the parabola of life and death and then descends the other. Europeanized and pragmatic like her brother, she ridicules the god Yangtze (here she embodies the scientific spirit ridiculing fate), calls for stones, cement and iron to subject death itself to man's service, indoctrinates the villagers, and tries to awaken her entire country to a spirit of self-improvement. But her brother is killed by their father, the dams break, the indoctrinated peasants are drowned. Mei-Ling is left with nothing except her individual dignity. All of her political endeavor has proved futile, and indeed she realizes the blindness and even cruelty that characterized her committed, political life. "Father," she cries, falling at Old Chiang's feet, "forgive me. Until this morning I was still very young, very cruel, deaf, blind, armed with hopes. But now at last I understand." She has finally surpassed hope, but she must also surpass despair, "conquering" fate by willing what it wills. This she does. But Mei-Ling's suicide is not just a personal exit, it is the definitive political act, a futile good deed that nevertheless affirms human solidarity because in giving herself she bequeaths a final hope to those unable to surpass hope and therefore unable to conquer fate in their own right. Thus her individual need for marriage with the abyss coincides with a wider social need: behind her affirmative suicide remains the double "cry" of individual dignity and communal solidarity.

Mei-Ling's complementary opposite, Old Chiang, reaches his salvation in an entirely different way — not through the quixotic activism of youth but through meditation and inner struggle. From the very start of the play, he has understood the vanity of all endeavor, though only theoretically, not experientially. His problem as the action unfolds and as the inhuman universe does its worse, is to struggle with the biological force which makes him naturally shrink from the metaphysical truths his mind has understood. Once again, we see the full parabola. Old Chiang is a complete man, his passivity and renunciation at the end acquiring validity because he has arrived at this Buddhistic acceptance of death by way of caring for life.

Though nominally the leader of a flock, he is treated in the play as the pure, unaccommodated, existential man: an isolated individual confronting the human condition. As the action progresses, he is stripped of everything that is meaningful to him in life until he is left completely alone with the Yangtze (Buddha). At first, his life has meaning because he is in a context extending backwards and forwards in time. He is the descendent of the all-powerful ancestors, the progenitor of the all-important progeny. He fears the former, places all his hopes in the latter, and lives in a seesaw world where the claims of one must be balanced against those of the other. At one point the ancestors weigh more heavily and at their behest he kills his son to appease the river, though he also takes steps to assure that his grandson will survive. From this point onward, Kazantzakis can take him up the various steps leading to salvation. He first learns to conquer his fear of the ancestors and, by extension, of the full domain of death represented by the Yangtze. Then he learns to conquer hope. In effect, he has no choice, for the plans laid for his grandson's escape go awry. Deprived of his cultural and human supports, without ancestors, son, daughter-in-law, grandson, daughter or kingdom, he remains in the pure existential situation, but this aloneness, together with his victory over fear and hope, opens the gate to salvation. How should he react at this point? What form of energy must be applied to the wheel of self to push it past this dead center? Kazantzakis's answer is clear. It is dignified acceptance. Whereas the common man screams, whimpers or runs imploringly to authority when he sees his death approaching, Chiang's response is lordly, displaying a quietude refined out of struggle. In him, spirit and body are not so much denied as conquered through the prowess of spirit and body. Because he has understood the self-deceiving nature of his efforts to achieve permanence, he is now — in a paradoxical way — above fate. Starting with an inherited, automatic philosophical position, he has transformed this theoretical position into an experiential one, earning the right to open his arms at the play's end and to welcome the flood (= Buddha). Now he truly knows that all of life's cares that we take so seriously are, beneath their deceptive multiplicity, a unified stream which is going where the waterfall is going: over the brink. This realization, this feat of human consciousness, gives him a pride and dignity that remain in the air as a cry after the universe has annihilated him. His Buddhism becomes strangely affirmative.

III

Though the play *Buddha* might strike some as nihilistic, it is not a pessimistic work, but rather a hymn to the pride and dignity not only of its characters but also of its author. What I claimed for Old Chiang can be claimed for Kazantzakis as well — namely, that his resignation becomes strangely affirmative because we feel that it has been earned. The play is not the expression of a man who was attempting to evade experience by passing it through the sieve of metaphysics, but of one who had been pushed by experience to question his assumptions all over again from the beginning and to emerge with a fresh consciousness of his relation to everything around him. In other words, it is the product of a man who had been pushed by experience to renewed and expanded self-consciousness. Kazantzakis would claim that human nobility lies precisely in this capacity for self-awareness and that self-awareness, furthermore, is the non-material goal of material evolution. The play gives artistic flesh and blood to these claims.

I have tried to show the comprehensiveness of *Buddha*, drawing attention to the Poet and Magician who serve as frame, to the action itself, with its upper and lower levels, and to how in each of these areas we are given the full parabola of life and death. I have also tried to indicate the experiences which lay in back of the play's prolonged gestation over several decades, culminating in Kazantzakis's exposure to his country's vicissitudes in 1940 and 1941. In writing the play, Kazantzakis attempted once more to synthesize the disparate aspects of himself, in particular his desire for political action versus his tendency toward philosophical resignation. He succeeded in this attempt by making activism the necessary precondition of a genuine futility. In other words: he justified activism in the short run because it places a crown of heroic dignity upon those who strive with open eyes, and in the long run because it leads to the non-material result of expanded self-consciousness.

Yet the ultimate solution presented by the play is the aesthetic one. All the foregoing is encased in art; imagination subsumes both politics and metaphysics. In this work, Kazantzakis does not trace the actual growth of the artistic position; he was to do this in his next book, *Zorba the Greek*, whose hero learns to deal with both activism and Buddhism by means of artistic creativity. In the play *Buddha* the artistic solution is already fully developed at the start — it is a given. By implication, however, we know that Kazantzakis felt that it, too, could be validated only after struggle, felt that active participation in life is the only path whereby imagination can earn the right to step back from life and treat it aesthetically with engaged aloofness. The artist accepts the unaesthetic as the necessary precondition of saving himself through the aesthetic.

These were the answers Kazantzakis arrived at in his renewed attempt, under the pressures of the events of 1940-1941, to reconcile the disparate aspects of himself (could we say "his deceptive multiplicity"?) and emerge with a coherent whole. The answers were not new; they are found in the *Odyssey* and other works. But of all of Kazantzakis's immense output, the play *Buddha* is the most straightforward in its exposition of his definitive position, because it so unapologetically presents the aesthetic as the primary way to salvation. A few months before he died, he told some Buddhist monks in China that of the three paths — meditation (metaphysics), good deeds (politics) and beauty (art) — he had followed the path of beauty. No wonder, then, that shortly before this he had declared: "*Buddha* is my swan song. It says everything. I'm glad that I have managed to utter…my final word in time, before I go."

[1]Letter to Elsa Lange, late August 1925, printed in Helen Kazantzakis, *Nikos Kazantzakis: A Biography* (New York, Simon and Shuster, 1968), pp. 125-6.

[2]Reprinted in *Japan China* (New York, Simon and Shuster, 1963), pp. 50-51. (George Pappageostes's translation, with some slight changes.)

[3]Translated into English by Kimon Friar as *The Saviors of God: Spiritual Exercises* (New York, Simon and Schuster, 1960).

[4]Mrs. Kazantzakis is certain that the only portion from an earlier version that survives in the final version is the episode of the two Greeks encountering Buddha. She also suspects that the second version, despite Kazantzakis's hopes for it, was destroyed or suppressed almost immediately — in any case before May 1924, when she and Kazantzakis first met. (Letter to Michael Tobias, March 16, 1982.)

CHARACTERS

The Poet

Buddha

Brahma

Siva

Vishnu

God of Wisdom

Temptation

Magician, (Hu-Ming) Buddha's disciple

Mogalana, Buddha's disciple

Saripoutta, Buddha's disciple

Hanna, Buddha's servant

Chiang, warlord

Old Man, Chiang's father

Li-Liang, Chiang's wife

Mei-Ling, Chiang's sister

Old Koag, the Old Man's head slave

Young Koag, monk, Old Koag's son

Mandarin, scribe

Markalo, Husband of Earth, an old man

Azure Butterfly, First Whore

Blossoming Cherry Tree, Second Whore

Fruit-Laden Lemon Tree, Third Whore

Moonglow, Fourth Whore

Li-Li-Foo, Fifth Whore

First Sentry

Second Sentry

Third Sentry

First Greek

Second Greek

Young Man

Moudita, his wife

Herald

First Musician, tambourine

Second Musician, drum

Third Musician, clarinet

First Soldier

Second Soldier

Third Soldier

The People

First Woman

Second Woman

Third Woman

First Man

Second Man

Third Man

First Old Man

Second Old Man

First Slave

Second Slave

First Disciple

Second Disciple

Third Disciple

Fourth Disciple

Peasant

Men and women both old and
young, peasants, soldiers,
servants, disciples

PROLOGUE

POET   Omnipotent Mind, merciless Father, you give birth to the sky,
land and sea, to the visible and invisible, to flesh and spirit;
You give them birth, love them and then blot them out —
Come, let us play.
My palms tingle; I long to grasp air, earth, water, fire — to
create. Heavy is my loneliness tonight;
Let me give life to the earth; let me open furrows that rivers
may run; let me build temples and palaces of air;
Let me adorn the wasteland with women, with peasants,
with gods, with monks, with noblemen.
I am tired; I am weary of loneliness; a sweet swoon saps my
strength this twilight.
I want to see and touch; I want to be seen and touched;
hands, eyes and mouths are what I long for,
And many shadows fighting, merging, parting, making
patterns in the wind.
O unborn spirits, be born! Spirits, take on flesh! Behold, I
stoop, take mud from the riverbank and knead.
The trough is good, the dough plenty and pliable, my palms
are deft, I pummel both men and gods.
Eh, Sun, stay and bake them!
(Bows to audience.)
My lords and ladies, welcome to my workshop this evening.
Open the eyes of your bodies and look; open the eyes of
your minds and see:
Behold, I tread on the land and level it out to create the
endless, tranquil land of China;
I cut the earth with my fingernail and open up a furrow for a
ribbon of water to enter and flow,
And it's the fearful, almighty river, the Yangtze. Bow down
and worship its grace.
I thrust a small stone into the clay and it becomes a majestic
tower with moats and bridges, battlements, stone gods and
many-colored, glowing lanterns.
I stoop and sift the lightest yellow porcelain clay, and blend it
with rosewater, nutmeg and cinnamon; I blow upon it and
shape lords and ladies, magicians, musicians and sages;
I take coarser clay, used for making jugs and pitchers, and

1

shape peasants and slaves, both male and female. At once
the shameless creatures move their hands, their feet, their
loins,
And long to couple.
Let them couple, we have plenty of earth and water; let's
shape guests as well; let a great festival burst across the
wasteland tonight
To while away the hours.
Men and gods, ethereal spring clouds, descend and take from
my hands the faces I give you;
Open your mouths; drink the holy communion of wine and
flame, the words I choose for you;
Don your festive nuptial garments; adjust your masks. The
Mind is to be married! Brightly adorn his bride, the Earth.
Let them come
Mounted on horses, waves, dreams, on great thoughts; let the
in-laws come,
Let bodies and spirits come!
Rise, O four winds, rise out of my temples; the sky overbrims
with stars; the earth overbrims with wheat.
Sift and winnow!
(The thick scrim lifts and the set appears: A Chinese village
with a square, a giant statue of Buddha in its center; on the
left, five bamboo huts; to the right, the great gate of the
Tower. In the rear, bowing in a row to the audience like
marionettes, are the principal players of the tragedy.)
Reverence and pity overwhelm me. What are these wisps of
smoke that have risen from the erect hairs of my head,
secured themselves to the air
And have become a village with statues and a tower?
What is this army of clay toys that has spilled out of my ten
fingers?
Open your hearts, your inner eyes, and look: They are not
clay toys, not wisps of smoke;
They are warm human beings, and each has a name, a bitter
history, an unbearable destiny.
They struggle like drowning mutes, opening and closing their
mouths in vain to cry: "Help! Help! Help!"
They are the ephemeral toys of the mind, azure wisps of
smoke above the wet plain.
O, mortals

2

I blow upon your earthen eyes to open them; I blow upon
    your earthen ears to open them; I blow upon your lips to
    warm them, to make them shout.
Lift up your heads, and look: Above the cobwebbed cellars
    of your existence rises the uppermost level of the world —
    weightless, full of light, thought, and smiles —
Buddha!
Listen! Behind the frenzied growl of the Yangtze, beyond the
    hoarse lament of drowning man
Buddha plays his flute sweetly, seductively, like a master-
    shepherd who at dusk invites the sheep into their pens.
The waters cry out in my entrails, the beasts speak, embassies
    of birds arrive in full dress; the gods descend with their
    begging bowls,
Buddha enters my head like a king entering his kingdom and
    the whole city creaks.
The unborn cling to the crags of my mind, burrowing into
    the subterranean passages of my heart; they don't want to
    leave.
Small children cry within me, women wail, beasts bellow,
    numberless birds cling to the tree of my entrails and warble:
"Father, give us a body, we are cold; give us a name, we are
    lost; give us a gender. We want to become male and
    female, to couple and give birth, so that we may not
    vanish.
Father, we yearn to suffer in earthen hands by loving, giving
    birth and dying.
Open the dark cage of your bowels; let us out!"
I stoop and press my ear to my breast; I hear humming within
    me, and I pity mankind.
I will unfurl a lightly-haunted tale, a yellow silken flag to
    declare war on suffering, ugliness and death.
Buddha! Buddha! Buddha!
I look to the North and South; I look to the East and West,
Buddha! Buddha! Buddha!
This world has no other consolation.
See how he stood and stretched out his hand quietly, without
    joy, without grief, then opened the door of nonexistence
And entered.
See how he turned his translucent head and bade the world
    farewell...how he spread his glance like a setting sun over

3

all people until, from head to toe,
They were dressed in saffron robes.
My children, a wind blows, ripening the buds on the trees,
and the world stirs. The secret Vine has risen out of my
bowels and entwines men, gods and ideas like shoots and
grapes.
The mountains glow like great thoughts; the starry sky
sways like a blossoming mandarin tree; the river Yangtze,
my broad royal vein, spills over my neck and refreshes me.
My children, shatter the iron bars of Necessity! Doff your
little earthen blouses; free the soul from the lime twigs of
the flesh,
For all is a dream; suffering, ugliness and death are illusions.
They do not exist.
Life is a game, death is a game — let's play awhile!
(Unhooks the gong.)
Let's play awhile! I unhook the gong from the abyss, strike it
three times to awaken the Imagination, that great bird
perched on the cliffs of my mind, and I cry.
(Strikes once and calls seductively. The curtain moves.)
Come!...Come!...Come!
(Strikes the gong a second time. Distant footsteps are
heard.)
He's coming...He's coming...He's coming...
(Strikes the gong a third time, hangs it up again, then steps
back. The Magician appears.)
Here he is!
(The Poet disappears.)

ACT I

(The Magician advances, dressed in the saffron robe of a Buddhist monk and wearing the mask of an old man. Two other masks hang from his neck.)

MAGICIAN   I've come. Three times I heard my name. Then a mysterious power — not at all mysterious, *my* power — stretched the wind taut, like a drum, from one end of the abyss to the other, then it sounded three times, and here I am.

Man must have need of me again. The fairy tale that conceals the truth must be torn and hanging like a rag again.

Man saw what was hiding behind it and became frightened. He cried out my name to the wind three times...
Help!...Help!...Help... Help is my name.

And here I am, with my unconquered army — the multi-colored, multi-winged, multi-eyed regiments of the imagination that fly over the dung heap called man's mind.

My army will destroy the breakwaters of the brain. It will disrupt and pillage all certainties.

I close the eyes of the body, I no longer see the ephemeral, I gaze on the eternal — a China reclining on clouds, made of water, sun and a gentle breeze.

She sails peacefully in the abyss with a prime wind, neither joyous nor sad, beyond time and place, beyond necessity.

I open the eyes of the body; instantly the eternal disappears, and I see before me a Chinese village beside the dreadful Blue River, the Yangtze,

Foul, muddy, filled with sweating men, pregnant women and swarms of children — it smells of human dung and of jasmine;

At the top of the village sits the Tower of the Master with its guffawing stone lions, foundations of seven times seven layers of bones, seven times seven layers of sighs from the slaves of the dreadful clan of Chiang.

At the foot of the Tower is a town square festively adorned with lanterns, myrtle and banners. In the center is a lightning-blasted, wild oak tree,

And the statue of Buddha with his four chins, four bellies, and four open doors leading to the fortress of his mind so the four winds might enter.

5

It's Buddha, Buddha; he looks at the people and bursts with
        laughter.
(*Young Koag, a slave, appears, dressed in a saffron robe. He
bows before the statue of Buddha, claps his hands, prays
softly, then hangs two silken lanterns to the right and left of
Buddha.*)

YOUNG KOAG   Buddha, Buddha, pity the people, pity the plants and animals,
        pity the stones, the waters and the soil.
    Blow upon the world, O Redeemer, and make it disappear.

MAGICIAN   (*Laughing softly.*)
    It's the beloved slave of the Master, Young Koag, with his
        doe-eyes and his long lashes.
    He's still too young to know how firm, sweet and full of
        essence the phantasmagoria of the world is.
    He hungers, thirsts and yearns, so he does not reach out his
        hand; he's ashamed and disgusted, yet he does not reach
        out his hand for food, wine, woman.
    This is not bread, he says; it is a chain that binds the soul
        with the body even more tightly, and God with filth. This
        is not wine, he says; it is the blood of Mara, of
        Temptation, that infects the blood of man with madness.
    This is not woman, he says; it is a building with cellars and
        sub-cellars, with open terraces over the precipice, with
        gardens and cesspools. It has an entrance, but no exit.
    Pity him, O souls who know the secret. His eyes, ears and
        mouth are still unopened buds. His life is still a heavy
        sleep in which he dreams of Buddha.
    But the hour has come. Tonight, woman will awaken him;
        his five senses will open and sprout leaves and flowers,
        and then bear round, downy, aromatic fruit —
    Death!
    Koag, eh Koag, our young monk!

YOUNG KOAG   (*Turns, murmuring with fear.*)
    The Magician!
    (*Falls to his knees in reverence.*)
    Command, O Lord!

MAGICIAN   What village is this, my young doe-eyed Koag?
YOUNG KOAG   O great Master of the rites of Buddha, you know. Why do
        you ask?

6

MAGICIAN	What holy day is this, doe-eyed Koag?
YOUNG KOAG	You know, Lord; why do you ask? You know all — past, present, future. You have three heads, Lord, and you see everything: what will be and what has been, the good, the evil, the visible and the invisible. You have three hearts, Lord; one pities, one mocks, and the third, the most compassionate, kills all things. You hold the strings Lord, and you control the Universe.
MAGICIAN	I do know all, Koag. Go, it's true, I have three hearts. The first pities and weeps; the second does not pity, it laughs; the third neither laughs nor weeps — it is silent. I hold three spools of string — white, red and black — and I control three paper kites with tassels and bells, with colored lanterns in the wind, the three great concepts — Life, Love, Death! I've brought all three spools with me tonight. A prime wind blows; I'll launch all three kites and entangle them in the murky air.
YOUNG KOAG	I kiss your feet, O great Master of the rites of Buddha. The moment has come; cut the strings that hold us to earth — the white, the red, the black, That we may be delivered.
MAGICIAN	*(Laughing.)* You are impatient, Doe-eyes, impatient…I like you…Go; I, too, am impatient. *(Koag bows and turns to leave.)* Koag!
YOUNG KOAG	Command me, Lord.
MAGICIAN	Are the players ready? Old Chiang? His son? His daughter? His daughter-in-law? The old Mandarin, the three musicians, the three sentries, the five whores? I need all these phantoms tonight, my young doe-eyed Koag.
YOUNG KOAG	All are ready, just as you commanded, Lord. They wait behind the curtains, costumed and painted, their hearts pounding and their ears cocked to hear your voice. When will you summon them, Lord?

7

MAGICIAN	When I wish. Go! And tell young Koag — my doe-eyed Koag — to be ready also. Do you hear? Ready, even to die.
YOUNG KOAG	I ask no other favor of you, Lord, but to die, to escape. I no longer want this world; pity me Lord, I no longer want it. I am like the butterfly that falls into the spider's web as that terrible weaver pounces upon it, swaddles its wings, wraps it round, and smothers it; So does the world entrap me...I am lost! Help me, Lord, to break my strings, to free my wings, to fly.
MAGICIAN	Patience, patience, my doe-eyed Koag; we shall soon reach salvation. Already I can feel the moist roots of the grass on your face. We are but a lightning's flash away, Koag, but do not fear, there is still time. I will thicken the spirit to make it flesh; I will thin the flesh to make it spirit. I will shatter the inner walls, confuse the elements, fit lion masks on rabbits. I will waken the people within God's bowels; I will play! I, too, have grown weary, Koag. The world moves too slowly, too sluggishly. We cannot wait for the seed to take root, to sprout leaves, buds, blossoms and fruit, and then to rot. We give the wheel and laggard time a push — seed and rot will become one. But you must help me, young monk of Buddha. Stretch out your hand and give the wheel a push; call the performers to assemble before me that I may give them my final instructions — how to speak, how to be silent, how to die... Do you hear, doe-eyed Koag?
YOUNG KOAG	I hear, Lord, and I obey. *(Bows and exits.)*
MAGICIAN	Wretched men...caught in the nets of flesh, they struggle to break free, to be saved...falling into even thicker nets, the nets of the Mind. And this they call Salvation! They merely exchange prisons — the walls are no longer of rocks, whitewash and iron bars, but of hopes and dreams. They exchange prisons, And they call this Freedom! *(Laughs.)* Let's change their prisons for them tonight!

8

(Looks around.)

Let's cast all cares aside! On this great festival tonight
the people will eat, drink and smoke hashish. The old
Master will descend from his Tower, the people will ascend
from the mud, and they'll all worship Buddha.

On a night like this, they say, Buddha untangled himself from
the nets of the flesh, slipped out of its five snares and found
invincible, immortal refuge —

He found Nothingness!

On a night like this, they say, Buddha left the world, escaped
from the conspiracy and ordered the five conspirators —
earth, water, fire, air and mind — to dissolve.

The humbly devout come tonight to see how the Chosen are
liberated, that they too, after thousands of incarnations,
after thousands of years, might one day find freedom.
What freedom?

Nothingness!

(Claps his hands and shouts.)

Eh! Eh! Eh!

*(The main characters enter and line up before him: Old
Chiang, Young Chiang, Mei-Ling, Li-Liang, the Mandarin, the
Three Musicians, the Three Sentries, the Five Whores. Behind
them, in a shapeless mass, is a crowd of people. Behind them,
the savage, muddy river, the Yangtze.)*

Welcome! Welcome! The moment has come, my children, for
you to show your skill before so many noblemen and ladies
this evening — don't disgrace me.

Art is a difficult task, a noble and dangerous balance over
the abyss; be careful.

Dance neither to the left, on the precipice of truth, nor to the
right, on the precipice of falsehood, but straight ahead,
across the abyss, upon the thin thread of freedom.

This dance is called Art.

Talk, laugh, cry, without the vulgar shouts and gestures of
foolish, living men. Subject the word, the smile, the tear,
to the stern, noble outline of human dignity.

Eh, old Chiang, do you understand? Come closer, don't be
afraid; you have much to wrestle with tonight — wrath,
love, pain — hang on tightly old Chiang, lest the Word
throw you.

You are the central pillar that supports the roof of my

9

imagination tonight — do not bend.

You are not the common people to whine and degrade yourself; you are not a god, a heart of stone, unable to feel pain, or love, or fear —

You are a nobleman, a lofty balance between the two precipices: the precipice of Man, and the precipice of God. You suffer, but you don't whine; you love and fear, but you don't degrade yourself. You look at the people and say, "I am to blame." You look at God and say, "No! I am not to blame; *You* are, but I assume the responsibility."

Eh, old Chiang, head-ram of my herd of shadows tonight, lead my fat ewes straight ahead toward the precipice; don't be frightened, do not change course.

This is the way, there is no other. Walk nobly to the end, for there lies salvation.

Rough, azure, full of flintstones is the path. And on the flintstones lie thick drops of blood.

It's not a precipice, old Chiang, it's not a precipice; it's salvation.

And you, young Chiang, condescend, take a step forward, come closer, irreverent soul of youth. You have no patience; you have no mercy. You hold the thunderbolt in your palm and you say:

"This is not a thunderbolt, it's a candle of peace; hang it in your homes to shine at night."

You are flesh of my flesh, you have no patience. You want to move the world in a day, to make it go further. I like you — strike!

O Mei-Ling, beloved, come forth; closer still, that I may touch you...what joy you gave me, joy and pride. I created you! Virgin lioness, you do not condescend to expend your strength on husband, friend or son; hold your head high my child, until the end.

It's a cruel fate to be pure, unsubduable, without faults; to scorn small joys, small virtues, small, sure truths.

To say: "I know a secret sweeter than life, more bitter than death. I know, but I tell no one, and I die for its sake."

Mei-Ling, you are a great, warm drop of my blood; my blessings upon you.

(Approaches, tenderly caresses Li-Liang.)

Li-Liang, wife of the fierce warlord Chiang, graceful and

soft-spoken, all passion, silence and nobility, companion of
    man,
I gaze upon you and my untamed heart grows tame; even at
    this late hour I can change the course of your destiny. I
    pity you, Li-Liang, I pity you, but I must not. Follow your
    fate, straight to the end, and let it take you where it may.
    This is the meaning of salvation.
Do not weep, unhappy girl; free yourself.
And you, musicians, sentries and whores; and you, old
    Mandarin with the gourd of wisdom on your shoulders;
    and you, workers, peasants and slaves, ballast of my ship;
And you, Blue River, blue-yellow, mud-covered mask that I
    will place tonight on the face of Destiny —
Take care! Are you ready?
I clap my hands, the performance begins!
(A canary sings. The Magician raises his head and listens
several minutes in ecstasy.)
Yes, yes, my canary, don't complain, I've not forgotten you,
    O pinnacle of freedom!
The omnipotent, mute powers are moving now to choke you.
    You still have a little time left, a little throat. Raise your
    head high and sing!
May the last voice heard above the waters that shall come to
    drown us be yours, O canary, O freedom! Sing!
And now, silence! Musicians, sit cross-legged in the corner,
    tune up your instruments, the tambourine, the drum, the
    clarinet; prepare yourselves.
Awaken the numberless, multi-colored birds that sleep in the
    dark throat of Nothingness.
Musicians, open the cage, the heart of man!
The wind is filled with sobbing, with erotic murmering, with
    laughter and signs of desperation: "Save our souls! Save
    our souls!" we shout. Onward, musicians, that we may
    finally hear our voices!
Good are the three keys you hold; the drum, the tambourine,
    the clarinet can open the abyss,
My heart has grown savage, I'm in a hurry! Leave, all of you!
    Let only these five whores remain.
(They leave. The three Musicians sit cross-legged in the
corner, at right. The five whores gaze in their little mirrors,
arranging their curls, painting their lips, as they walk toward

11

the Magician.)

Welcome! Welcome, deflated secrets, communal fountains at
the crossroads, O doors to Paradise open day and night,
wider even than the bowels of God,

Where ascetics and criminals enter—gay, young blades and
hunchbacks, beggars and kings—

Where all receive communion.

O five, welcoming sacred Doors: Azure Butterfly, Blossoming
Cherry-Tree, Fruit-Laden Lemon Tree, Moonglow, and
you, sweet-kissing Li-Li-Foo,

Come forward, the blessed hour is here; raise to your lips
the words I buried in your hearts; unwind all the deeds I
wound up for you.

O, five, great martyrs of love, cast a farewell glance in your
little mirrors, paint a final beauty mark on your small
cheeks, prepare yourselves. The performance begins. In the
name of God!

*(The five Whores run to their bamboo huts where they
hurriedly primp.)*

Oh! Oh! The little women of love come and go, shaking their
behinds like fatted ewes.

They've hurriedly unfolded their overworked beds and hung
their multi-colored lanterns, and now, here they are,

Dressing, adorning themselves, dousing themselves with
perfumes so they won't stink; and they stand like a ship's
figurehead freshly painted, their hands crossed beneath
their accommodating, hanging breasts, two communal
fountains,

Waiting for men.

It has snowed on the high mountains; it has rained, it has
rained forty days and forty nights on the plain. It has
rained, and the Blue River, the Yangtze, has swollen. It
leaps and rams its banks to knock them down, to drown
the world.

Let men open their ears. The soft hum of their laughter, their
quarrels, their crying children, and their boiling pots drown
out

The mighty roar of the Yangtze

But I hear one thing only, not women, or babies, or pots; I
hear one sound only:

The mighty Roar. I roar, too, like the Yangtze, and I descend!

12

I can hold back no longer; I will open the ears of my father,
my son and my friend to hear the Yangtze descending, to
hear a hoarse voice leaping out of the soil: "We are lost!
We are lost!"
Let them awaken!
(Whistles seductively and calls softly.)
Blossoming Cherry-Tree, enticing songstress, come closer,
begin, sing!
Passion has made you lean, my Blossoming Cherry-Tree, and
you sigh, because you have fallen into sin. What sin?
You have crammed the Creator into one creature, infinity
into one body;
You chose one among men, young Koag, doe-eyed Koag, and
you said:
"It's him I want, not the others. It's for him I dress and
undress, it's for him I sing."
What a shame; you stopped the masks that roll over the face
of Destiny, and you said: "Let all masks be gone; let only
this one remain."
Rise up now, and pay for your sin.
But first, before you are killed, sing.
I want to hear the song you dislike, the one I rubbed violently
on your lips, like honey.
Sing, Blossoming Cherry-Tree.
(Sings enticingly:)
"Dear God, put out the sun, or I'll be lost..."

BLOSSOMING   (Dressed in a kimono embroidered with a branch of a
CHERRY TREE   blossoming cherry tree, sunk in lethargy, she listens to the
                    Magician. Gradually her face comes alive, she is carried
                    away, claps her hands and begins to sing.)
                    "Dear God, put out the sun, or I'll be lost..."

MAGICIAN   Sing louder; stop shaking your hips so shamelessly; you've
                    entered the sacred forest of art; walk with reverence.

BLOSSOMING   Dear God, put out the sun, or I'll be lost;
CHERRY TREE   descend, O night, at length that I may rest
                    and lie in bed alone;
                    all day long in the streets I hawk my wares
                    and to all, old and poor, I sell my bare
                    young body, flesh and bone.

13

What may the eyes see when they open wide?
But when I close my lashes tight, inside
what happiness awakes,
for then a dream, a doe, leaps into sight
and fills my aching, empty arms with pride,
with downy, curly locks.

Dresses of rustling silk then shall I wear
and douse myself with perfumes, and with care
besprinkle my beloved beau,
as over us the cherry trees will bloom,
the black-eyed hours then will cease too soon,
and in our village — O,

dear God, let not one sound of crowing burst
in air, nor let the sun, may it be cursed,
rise with the cocks at dawn,
but let each lovely lass sleep, ring on ring,
a deathless, charming and enchanting spring,
with lads on every lawn.

(Turns uneasily toward the Magician.)

MAGICIAN
    You sang well. Don't tremble, Blossoming Cherry-Tree; don't tremble, or all your blossoms will fall to the ground.
    And now, light your red lantern, it's dark; hang it by your door,
    My little firefly.
    (Whistles invitingly.)
    Eh, Fruit-Laden Lemon Tree, it's your turn! Come here, angry girl, don't be afraid of me, scold me. I speak with your lips; don't tremble. You are merely the reed
    On which I blow and play whatever tune I please.
    And you, beloved Li-Li-Foo, go inside, unfold your mattress, douse your bedsheets with rosewater, open your kimono,
    I'm coming!
    (The whore leaps angrily towards the Magician, wearing a kimono embroidered with fruit-laden lemon-tree branches, shaking her hands menacingly.)
    Splendid! Frown more with your eyebrows; place your hands on your hips, scream! Do you remember the words, "Eh, monk, for shame"? That's how you begin...

Courage, Fruit-Laden Lemon Tree, it's not you who speak, I
tell you; it's I who speak with your lips. Don't be afraid.

FRUIT-LADEN
LEMON TREE

Eh, monk, for shame! Lift your eyes across to the holy
mountain; cock your ears to the air;

Those flames are not fires lit by shepherd boys, those are not
sheepdogs barking, monk, it's your Monastery burning!
The monks are leaping in the flames; their saffron robes
have caught fire.

A demon, you know the one — his tongue is fire — has seized
your monastery in his claws and he's licking it!

Rise, monk, they say your power is great, that you hold
magic and thunderbolts in the palm of your hand. Rise
and fight!

Why do you stroll here and spin the air? Rise and fight!

You know it's not a demon; it's Chiang, Chiang, son of the
Tower Master, may he be cursed!

MAGICIAN

It's not Chiang, it's not Chiang, it's hoarfrost. It's not a
monastery, it's hoarfrost.

Stop shouting, Fruit-Laden Lemon Tree, everything is
hoarfrost. Even Buddha himself is hoarfrost, but he knows
it —

That's why he's Buddha.

Don't frown. Everyone in this world performs his duty well,
very well. You comb your hair, shake your hips, simp
and smirk, glue a smile on your face, and then wait for men.

The Nobleman inside his tower eats, drinks, holds Injustice
on his knees, caresses her and rejoices —

He caresses Injustice and the world appears just to him, and
God a firm Tower — his tower.

And out there, as you say, the valiant fight for hoarfrosts
and phantoms; they fight and are killed — good for them!
And I sit here — good for me! — and spin the air.

All's well, Fruit-Laden Lemon Tree, all the actors are in their
places —

The Blue River, the Monastery, the Tower, the Master, the
People — and Death.

All the actors are in their places; the performance will go
well tonight. Light your lantern, too, Fruit-Laden Lemon
Tree; the words I placed on your lips have ended, go!

It's your turn, Azure Butterfly.

15

AZURE BUTTERFLY   (*Turns toward the statue of Buddha.*)
I raise my arms, I clap my hands, I cry out: "Buddha,
    Buddha,
(*Pointing to the Magician.*)
Blow upon this shameless structure of bones and flesh that
    it may rot!
He has no shame, no fear, he has gone beyond the boundaries
    of man. He's no longer man, but he's not yet a demon,
    he's somewhere in the middle. This is the moment, Buddha
    — kill him!"
(*To the Magician.*)
What performance, monk? For shame! Tonight you must
    conduct a great liturgy: the people and the nobles have
    trembled all year long, anxiously waiting for this night —
Bring God down from the heavens, raise the souls of the
    Ancestors from the earth, break our bodies, the thick-
    skinned husks of our souls;
Then all of us, slaves and masters, gods and men, the living
    and the dead, shall become one.
It's a terrible moment, thrice-blessed holy man; it's your duty,
    monk, to draw your mind away from food, drink and
    women, that you may fight
With that untamed element, the miracle.
But your lordship has come dressed in silk like a bridegroom.
    Instead of a sword, you hold a quill; instead of a shield,
    two masks hang from your neck; and you are not ashamed
    on such a night as this
To squander your strength on women.

MAGICIAN   How else, my Azure Butterfly, how else can I gain
    momentum? If I fall upon food, I become heavy, I cannot
    walk — and it's my great duty to dance.
If I fall upon great thoughts, I whirl like fire; I am hurled
    into the sky; I play tenpins with the clouds; and woe to
    the heart on whom the lightning bolt falls!
Woman sits in the middle between food and great thoughts.
    She sits with bared breasts and open knees,
And I touch her...I touch her,
And lo, what can it be, my Azure Butterfly, what can this
    mystery be, my Fruit-Laden Lemon Tree? The moment I
    touch her, then weight and whirlwind mingle divinely

16

within me,
And I dance!

MOONGLOW   (Laughing.)
Come then, my dancer — dance with me. Look, I have bathed,
    combed my hair, bared my breasts.
I am a woman, and I, too, sit, as you say, between food and
    great thoughts and open my knees — come here and refresh
    your strength.

MAGICIAN   The smelt needs octopus as bait, the mullet needs cheese, the
    male cuttlefish a female cuttlefish. Every form of life on
    land and sea, as you know, has its own bait, and is caught.
    By God's will, every man has his own woman as bait, and
    he nibbles.
Forgive me, Moonglow, I will go to the hut of my old friend,
    Li-Li-Foo
To nibble a little.
(Walks slowly towards Li-Li-Foo's hut, then turns to the
Musicians.)
Eh, Musicians, tambourine, drum, clarinet, why do you stand
    there and gape at me? The performance has begun, let
    your hearts go!
Words reach as far as the door of Paradise, but they can't
    enter. The Mind pounds on the door of Paradise, shouts
    that it's the great Nobleman, the Mind, but the door won't
    open.
Yet when music comes, it filters in through the cracks.
Drum, tambourine, clarinet — say now what words have no
    power to say. The time has come for my terrifying shout to
    rise out of the earth.
Until then, I go to woman to refresh my strength.
(Unloosens his belt, puts on the black-bearded mask that
hangs on his chest and enters the hut of Li-Li-Foo. The
Musicians play a savage, muffled tune for a long while.
Suddenly out of the bowels of the earth a serpent's strong
hissing and a harrowing cry are heard: "We are lost!" The
music stops abruptly. The Four Whores dash out of their
huts, frightened.)

AZURE BUTTERFLY   Did you hear? Did you hear? Fs-s-s-s, like a serpent…We're
    lost!

BLOSSOMING CHERRY TREE	Yes, yes, I heard...we're lost! *(Falls to the ground, covering her ears.)*
FRUIT-LADEN LEMON TREE	Why are you trembling, Blossoming Cherry-Tree, my little sister? *(Suddenly terrified.)* Do you think it was...?
BLOSSOMING CHERRY TREE	Yes, yes, it was, it was! I know their voices...I'm afraid.
MOONGLOW	The Ancestors?
BLOSSOMING CHERRY TREE	Yes, yes, the Ancestors...The Ancestors are calling from under the earth. They've opened their earth-filled mouths and are crying out. What do they want now? Haven't the gluttons had enough? Of all the bountiful blessings men bring us from God in payment for a kiss, we, poor wretches, Who work all night, give them their share every morning — Rice, honey, wine. And what do *they* do, the parasites? Do they stand on their doorsills calling out to customers like magpies, craw, craw, craw? Do they kiss, lie awake and expend themselves all night long? Do they brim with saliva, sweat, pinches, cigarette burns, stench from wine-soaked breaths, from spit, from filth, Like garbage pails? No, no, the masters lie in the cool earth, open their bottomless mouths two spans wide, and shout, "Hey, you living, we want food! Hey, you living, we want wine!" And we go, poor souls, filling their earthen pots as they eat and stuff their bellies. Eh, enough! The dead eat too much; let them eat us too, and so release us! Let's also become the dead — to eat up the living!
BLOSSOMING CHERRY TREE	They're not hungry, they're not thirsty, Fruit-Laden Lemon Tree. Don't you hear them? They're afraid.
AZURE BUTTERFLY	Are they afraid of a night like this? Of Buddha's festival when all the passions — hunger, thirst, fear — become light and turn into air?
MOONGLOW	Oho, Chiang must have dug up the bones from the Monastery graves, Chiang, excommunicated Chiang,

18

And the souls have dispersed in the wind and now weep.

FRUIT-LADEN   *(Placing her ear to the ground.)*
LEMON TREE   Listen...Listen...Hoards of moles are running...and
               screeching...

AZURE BUTTERFLY   No...no...It's not moles you hear...It's not our Ancestors...
                   Oho, it's —
                   (Jumps up terrified.)
                   It's the waters running...waters, waters, waters under the
                   earth.

BLOSSOMING   The waters! Do you think it could be...We're lost!
CHERRY TREE

MOONGLOW   Oh! Oh! Could it be...?

FRUIT-LADEN   Who? Who?
LEMON TREE

ALL THE WHORES   The Yangtze?
                  *(Terrified, the four crumple to the floor. Music filled with
                  fear is heard. Three young monks wearing saffron robes
                  appear. They bow in reverence to the statue of Buddha and
                  decorate it with flowers, chanting softly.)*

THREE MONKS   Like a silkworm, Buddha has anchored
               on the boughs of unflowering silence;
               he's eaten all the leaves,
               he's eaten all the leaves of earth's mulberry tree,
               he's eaten all the leaves and turned them into silk!

BLOSSOMING   *(Bursting into tears.)*
CHERRY TREE   He's eaten all the leaves...He's eaten all the leaves...Oh, a
                   caterpillar is eating
               The leaves of my heart.
               Buddha, Buddha, I'm not ready yet; all my flesh has not
                   become spirit yet; I hunger, I hurt, I love, I still want to
                   kiss.
               You know my secret, Buddha,
               Take away the grace you've given me; I don't want it
                   anymore!
               Take it away! I don't want
               Salvation!

19

MOONGLOW	Let her cry, she'll feel better; what would we poor women do without tears?
	She's remembering her little Koag, doe-eyed Koag, and she's crying.
	(Runs to the first hut and shouts:)
	Li-Li-Foo! Li-Li-Foo!
AZURE BUTTERFLY	Moonglow, why are you calling her? Hush!
MOONGLOW	She knows many spells; let her cast her spells on the demons in the air so we'll find relief.
FRUIT-LADEN LEMON TREE	*(Scornfully.)*
	What spells? She knows only one, the one that enslaves men: "Command me!" Nothing more.
	She's sly, she won't say, "I want!" She's shameless, she won't say, "Come!" She's a wheedling whore, she won't say, "Give me!" She only says, "Command me!" and she enslaves men.
	(Laughter is heard from the first hut.)
BLOSSOMING CHERRY TREE	Who's with her? Who's she laughing with? Her hut is shaking ...Li-Li-Foo
	(To Fruit-Laden Lemon Tree.)
	Why are you laughing, Fruit-Laden Lemon Tree?
FRUIT-LADEN LEMON TREE	She's in all the nine heavens now; how can she hear you? If you open her door, you'll see on her mattress a strange beast with four feet, four hands, two heads and forty claws.
MOONGLOW	Is she with her lover, the Magician?
	Don't be sinful, hush! The Magician will conduct the liturgy tonight; he'll present the Holy Passions of Buddha in this very square.
	He must not touch food or wine or woman for three days and nights. He must keep his mind clear and light; he must rise above the clouds and look down from there upon the world crawling in the mud like a worm.
	He must see it, pity it, then fit it with wings that it may escape.
FRUIT-LADEN LEMON TREE	I saw him I tell you; I saw him with my own eyes. He's full of food and wine, and he smells like a he-goat...
	He carries a long blue feather like a shepherd's crook and

20

	goads the spirits on.
AZURE BUTTERFLY	How did you recognize him? He can become a youth, a mature man, an old man, whatever he wants to be. Around his neck he wears the three fundamental faces and keeps interchanging them — and no one knows his real face.
	Eh, Musician, beat the drum louder! Louder! Louder, till it breaks!
	(The door of the Tower opens abruptly. An old and a young man rush out, holding whips. The music stops.)
	It's old Koag, the Master's head-slave,
MOONGLOW	And his son, doe-eyed Koag.
	(Holds on to Blossoming Cherry-Tree so as not to fall.)
	Blossoming Cherry-Tree...
BLOSSOMING CHERRY-TREE	*(Looking with longing at young Koag.)*
	How pale he is...He's melting away...Buddha licks you like a lion and eats your face away, my boy...
	(The young man bows, pays homage to Buddha, and prays silently in deep meditation.)
	He's going to take him away from me...he, Buddha, Buddha, let me, also, complete all my cycle. Let me kiss, let me have my fill that I may be liberated...don't take him from me.
	(Rushes toward the young man, but old Koag cracks his whip in the air and she stops, terrified.)
OLD KOAG	The Master wants silence. Silence!
	(Turns toward young Koag.)
	He's kneeling before the Ancestors; he's praying.
	He's bathed and adorned himself; he's put on his huge wings, and he's talking now with the Ancestors.
	Cross your hands, musicians; close your mouths, women; silence!
	Like a torrential rain, prayer erodes the soil, softens rocks, opens furrows and descends into the deep graves;
	The white skulls rise, ears grow back again and listen — be quiet, so that they may hear the words of the Master.
YOUNG KOAG	Patience, my sisters; salvation approaches...The sun is setting; soon the full moon will rise over the fields. Masters and

people will merge,
And the liturgy will begin.

BLOSSOMING
CHERRY TREE
My brother, doe-eyed Koag, turn your eyes and look at me;
stretch out your hand and pity me. Pity me, my boy;
give me your lips to quench my thirst.

If you allow me to lie under the earth with my thirst still
unquenched, you'll carry a great sin on your head,
doe-eyed Koag,

For I will be born again, and you'll be to blame; I'll
wander from body to body — and you'll be to blame — that
I may find you, kiss you, that I may be liberated. Don't
you pity me?

Hasten my liberation!

YOUNG KOAG
My sister, Blossoming Cherry-Tree, lower your eyes, close
your lips and listen: Sweet is the evening, compassionate,
mute, like the last evening of the world —

Don't contaminate it.

BLOSSOMING
CHERRY TREE
Doe-eyed Koag, if this is the last evening of the world, then
throw away the whip you're holding. What do you need it
for?

Sweeten your lips, perfume your hair, I've opened my arms
for you, come!

YOUNG KOAG
O Buddha, stretch out your hand and heal this woman.
She's sick, sick; she thinks of nothing else but kisses. Heal
her!

(Stoops and chants softly.)

When will this sack, my body, become exhausted,
when will the tears that choke me flow away,
when will this earth sprout wings and be entrusted,
O Buddha, to fly away?

(Turns to Blossoming Cherry-Tree.)

When will you, too, Blossoming Cherry-Tree, sing those
words of the holy prostitute Vimala, who donned the
saffron robe?

BLOSSOMING
CHERRY TREE
When I am old, when my teeth, my breasts and my hair have
fallen. My body's still a beast that wants to eat. I stretch
out my hand;

22

Have mercy on me, young Koag,

YOUNG KOAG   I stretch out my hand, sister, have mercy on me! Yesterday I
             cut my hair and laid it at the feet of Buddha; tomorrow I'll
             go crawling into the Monastery like a worm, to knit my
             cocoon, to work on my wings;
Don't obstruct my salvation.

OLD KOAG   Silence! Silence! The Master wants silence. Eh, ladies with
             the little white teeth, come near, here's a piece of mastic
             to chew on so your mouth will smell sweetly,
So it won't cry out.
*(The two Koags enter the Tower. The four women sit cross-
legged in front of their huts.)*

AZURE BUTTERFLY   Let's sit crosslegged on the ground; let's make our eyebrows a
                  little larger; let's make our curls fall over our ears.
Men grow crazy and scatter-brained when they see us, and
                  they open their hearts and their purses.

BLOSSOMING   *(Passionately.)*
CHERRY-TREE   I don't want to! I don't want to!
                  *(She dishevels her hair, breaks her combs, tears off the
                  flowers at her breast, takes dirt and smudges her face.)*
                  I don't want to!
                  *(Terrifying music suddenly bursts forth. A cry is heard
                  again, as though from the depths of the earth: "We are lost!")*

ALL THE WOMEN   *(Stretching out their arms in fear to Buddha.)*
                  Help! Help, Buddha!
                  *(The Magician appears in Li-Li-Foo's doorway, girds himself
                  slowly, removes the manly mask and becomes an old man
                  again. He looks at the wailing women and laughs.)*

MAGICIAN   *(Pointing to Buddha.)*
                  Are you asking him for help? Him? Never!

MOONGLOW   Don't laugh, can't you hear the Ancestors calling? Don't you
                  hear them calling from under the earth?

MAGICIAN   Close your shell-pearled ears, my ladies, so you won't hear
                  them. The Ancestors do not speak to women,
They speak to men.

BLOSSOMING CHERRY-TREE	But we hear their voices too.
MAGICIAN	Sing, laugh, jingle your bracelets so you won't hear their voices.
	Men hear and reply; mercy on the world if women begin to reply too. Your daily wage in the world is of another kind, it's sweeter.
	Li-Li-Foo! Laugh, my wagtails, laugh I say! Throw your arms around men, don't listen to the earth!
	Li-Li-Foo!
LI-LI-FOO	(*Appears, and bows.*)
	Command me!
MAGICIAN	Beloved Li-Li-Foo, wash my feet; they have a long way to go tonight. Bring me perfumes; I shall ascend and talk to the spirits. If I smell of human sweat, they'll not come near me.
	Bring me tea to drink, so my mind may waken from its numbness, and may spread out its net from the top of my head down to my heels. There are many fish it will catch tonight, goldfish and dogfish!
	(*Li-Li-Foo bows, enters the hut. She reappears shortly, bringing tea. Then she kneels and washes his feet.*)
	Li-Li-Foo, I like you. You speak only two words, the most feminine of all, the most powerful: "Command me!"
	Woman needs nothing more.
BLOSSOMING CHERRY-TREE	I bow, monk, and worship the shadow of your head; How do you know the secrets of women so well, monk?
MAGICIAN	In another life, I, too, was a compassionate working woman like you.
	I, too, lugged a mattress on my back from villages to cities, shouting, "Kisses, sweet kisses for sale! Eh, soldiers, merchants, sea captains, peasants, workers, craftsmen, apprentices, I sell kisses — first come, first served!"
	But enough, get ready, you too have much to do tonight, many bodies to drown in honey.
	(*The women scatter and light the lanterns, singing softly.*)
	Night has fallen, I'm hungry. Night has fallen and I'm off to the hunt. Like lions, like rhinoceri, like scorpions, the words of Buddha stalk the forest.
	(*He sniffs the air, holds his nose.*)

Mildew, mould, filth, and flesh that hasn't seen the sun. I sniff
the air; Wisdom strides over the earth and approaches,
that coarse nanny with her hanging dugs filled with ink...
A hundred-year-old baby with white eyebrows has clambered
into her arms, and suckles.
It suckles from above, sucks red, black, blue and purple inks,
then excretes them and befouls its diapers with letters...
Its nanny crows with pride, changes the baby's diapers. It
befouls them once more.
It befouls them again and again, leaving behind it *The
Chronicles of Man.*
He's coming, he's coming...here's the old Mandarin, the aged
baby of Wisdom.
*(The old Mandarin appears, out of breath, holding a huge
notebook under his arm.)*

MANDARIN   I've clambered up, panting, to the village square of insanity,
for here tonight the impious Magician will break the laws;
he'll get Necessity drunk, he'll topple the world into chaos
again;
He'll prod that multi-colored army of insanity, the miracles.
He'll scatter in a moment all I've weighed, arranged and
locked up in the chests of my mind these many years. All
that in thousands of years the Ancestors have built with
hammer, trowel and stone,
This man, with a long feather held aloft, will topple.
He builds the foundation of men's houses with clouds.
Instead of placing a brain in man's head to measure with, to
weigh all things well, to write with, this elf-brained fool
places a canary.
But tonight I can't bear it any longer. Here in this wide
village square of insanity
I've brought with me, under my armpit, *The Chronicles of
Man.*
I shall fight!

MAGICIAN   Oh welcome to our wise Mandarin, the fearless skipper of
our walnut shell!
Your fleet is a walnut shell and sails into open waters to
attack.
Your God is a clown who holds paper and pen, sits on the
pier, watches the ships coming and going, and writes:

25

"All are mine!"

He hears the cocks crowing, the goats and sheep scrambling downhill, the fortresses banging away, and he writes:

"All are mine!"

He's dying of hunger and thirst, so he sits and writes "Bread!" and his hunger is appeased. He writes "Wine!" and he becomes drunk. He writes "Woman!" and he fathers children.

A thousand welcomes to the wise Mandarin with the round, buzzing pumpkin on his shoulders! He's ill, poor soul, he's ill; he's come out with a large boil, look at it!

A large boil under his armpit!

MANDARIN   This isn't a boil, bird-brain; this is *The Chronicles of Man.* Don't laugh! I've lugged it here with me tonight to read it to the Master and the people,

To bring the people you want to lead astray back to the right path; to cut the wings you want to plant on them tonight; to open their eyes so they may see

How man has fought, worked and conquered on earth, how he has not walked with wings,

But with feet!

(Coughs, his knees give way and he sits down cross-legged.)

MAGICIAN   *(Helps him to lie on the ground, laughing.)*

His legs aren't strong, his loins are weak, his phallus has shrunk to a raisin...Eh, don't laugh, he's the God of Wisdom.

MANDARIN   Haven't you any respect for man's labors? Can't you face truth without bursting into laughter? You scramble up the heads of men

And crow like a rooster.

MAGICIAN   Hold your tongue, Wisdom, your nakedness is showing; the head has seven holes — close all of them.

Old man, we've come to the edge of the precipice — jump!

MANDARIN   You talk, you laugh, you hold a cup and drink tea, but your hand doesn't tremble, as though you haven't heard...

Haven't you heard? We're lost!

MAGICIAN   I know.

MANDARIN   It's Chiang, Chiang, the cursed general...

MAGICIAN   I know. I know. I know everything!

MANDARIN   Then how can you laugh? My God, where do you get the strength to play?

MAGICIAN   I pretend I don't know, you old codger. I live, eat, sleep, kiss, drink tea, as though I don't know.
That is my strength.
You see, I can't stop the river Yangtze from descending, I can't change the world I see — death, ugliness, shame, vulgarity, cowardice — I can't; but it's not even necessary.
There's only one thing I can change, one thing only, but that is enough.

MANDARIN   What is that?

MAGICIAN   The eye that sees the world. I change the eye, and the world changes — this is the great secret,
This is my magic.

MANDARIN   You're the cock of the earth with long feathers and — forgive me — little wisdom. Have you thought to ask me? I'm half blind from studying *The Chronicles of Man*.
Here, here.
(Leafs through notebook.)
It's written here in large red letters: "Every time the Yangtze overflows and drowns the world, the Ancestors leap from their graves and shout: 'We are lost! We are lost!' and they weep."
Don't laugh, gather your wits together and listen.
(Leafs through and reads:)
"To the glorious dynasty of Song, during the reign of..." The worm's eaten a word here "...of the king...
The Yangtze overflowed, broke the dams, drowned four hundred villages and forty large..." The mice have eaten a word here — must be "cities" — "forty large cities. And when the waters receded, they left on the fields a sediment of sand and bones the height of three men..."
Do you hear, cock of the earth? Sand and bones! This is what I read, and my heart breaks.

MAGICIAN   *(Laughing.)*

Aren't you ashamed, wise old man? Were you frightened?
Haven't you yet learned man's long history? Hasn't your
heart turned to stone by now?

MANDARIN   To stone?

MAGICIAN   No, not stone, it crumbles. Nor iron, it rusts, Air!

MANDARIN   Air?

MAGICIAN   *(Laughing.)*
Your heart is still an inkwell. Well then, carry your penknife
    about, whittle your reed pen, grind your black paint,
    prepare new ink, fill up your heart and write!
There's a great festival tonight; I'll launch a many-colored
    kite in the wind, with small bells, lanterns and a tassled
    tail — my mind!
Prick up your ears, old penpusher; listen to what I say and
    write, write,
Then take your writings, make them a paper boat and toss it
    into the river
(Sarcastically.)
To bring the news to future generations.
Ah, ah, if only the waterworms knew how to read, how they
    would laugh down in the mud, at the bottom of the river!
This is how airbrained man launches his soul; he shapes it
    into a paper boat, draws God on it as skipper — and then
    tosses it into the abyss.

MANDARIN   Laugh, laugh, airbrained bird of the wind! But I don't hold a
    feather, like you; I hold a scale and I weigh; I weigh, and
    I've found...

MAGICIAN   What have you found?

MANDARIN   That we're lost!

MAGICIAN   The little worm holds a scale and weighs the universe. But the
    true wise man, O penpusher, doesn't hold a scale; he
    doesn't hold notebooks; he holds a fan made of peacock
    feathers
And he fans the air! And then he thinks, without sweating
    under his armpits, that we're all lost!
Don't shout; look at Buddha and struggle to be like
    him. Do

28

you know why he laughs?

MANDARIN   No.

MAGICIAN   I know. If I tell you, you'll fall flat on your back with fear.
His laughter goes beyond wisdom, beyond insanity, beyond
boundaries, to the other shore.
Don't ask, you won't be able to bear it. Woe to the man who
wants to undress truth and see her nakedness! He is
blinded, not at all by her beauty, but
By fear!
(A distant roar is heard, as of waters rushing.)

MANDARIN   Listen, listen to the river! It has swelled, it's become angry, it
bellows like a beast. I must leave.

MAGICIAN   Where will you go? All roads are blocked. He's come, the
Uninvited Guest has come. Don't leave, don't degrade
yourself; dip your reed pen into your heart, and write.
What month is it?

MANDARIN   April.

MAGICIAN   What day?

MANDARIN   The 23rd of April.

MAGICIAN   Write! Not on the first pages, my old man; don't you
understand yet? Here, here on the last page, in the
epilogue. Write: "On the 23rd of April, at the festival of
Buddha, when old Chiang was Master, with the blue
dragon on his banner,
When the moon was full, when the heavens opened and
merged with the earth, when it rained and rained and
rained for forty days and forty nights —
It was then the world sank."
Courage old man, don't be afraid, it's nothing...
It's nothing; it's only Death.

MANDARIN   Gather your wings, accursed, rapacious vulture, shut your
mouth — the people are coming.
Pity them, don't pounce upon them!
*(The people arrive, the terrified old men in front. Behind are
the peasants with their tools; further back, the women. The
whores run to their doorsteps and call out to the old men.)*

29

FRUIT-LADEN LEMON TREE	Eh, old men, we have eternal water here. Look! *(Bares her breasts.)* Two refreshing springs; come and drink!
MOONGLOW	Come and drink, and your hair will turn black again, your mouths will fill with teeth again!
AZURE BUTTERFLY	They can't hear, they're old; they don't thirst, they're old. Their minds are on Buddha.
MAGICIAN	*(To the Mandarin.)* Write! *(Cross-legged, the Mandarin listens and writes. The old men have escaped the whores, encircled the statue of Buddha, and have raised their hands.)*
OLD MEN	*Buddha, with your large earrings, you who keep* *your watch on land and sea, devoid of hope,* *who cast the leaves of mulberry tree to cope* *with human worms that creep,*
	Help us, O help! The dead stir in the earth, *the ground has cracked, and in its deep ravines* *all human skulls have broken through and seem* *to clack their mouths in mirth.*
	Buddha, you have a thousand, thousand hands *of fierce revenge, of hunger, and of rage,* *of sweetness and hope, of silence that from its cage* *of stars falls on our lands,*
	and of a great, wild scorn. Pity our nation, *pity all men now on this holy night* *and over their hearts spread out from a great height* *the hand of your compassion.*
	(The men arrive, angry. They carry weapons which they throw with rage to the ground.)

FIRST MAN	Buddha, Buddha, listen to our sins, take them with you,
	    throw them into oblivion! Look,
	I turn my heart upside-down at your feet, wash it, and rinse
	    it in the river — and I reject Chiang! I throw down my
	    weapons and reject the son of Chiang. I reject the gods he
	    brought us

30

From the white demons.

SECOND MAN   I will tear down the factories he built, and the schools, and
              the baths; I will burn the railroads, the telephones, the
              telegraphs, the automobiles. I will fall again before the
              magicians, the exorcists, the astrologers,
              And beg them to sell me the wind, that I may travel; to
              advise me where to build my home so the spirits won't tear
              it down; where to dig my parents' grave so they won't
              come back to haunt me;
              And how to embrace my wife so the demons won't deform
              my seed inside her womb.

THIRD MAN   Buddha, Buddha, look, we throw Chiang's weapons at your
              feet; we don't want to fight and more; we shout:
              "Buddha, put out your hand, stop the Yangtze! Stop the
              Yangtze, Buddha, don't let it drown us!"

MAGICIAN   *(Softly, to the Mandarin.)*
              Don't write that down, old man; do me the favor and don't
              write it down. They're people, little people, let them shout.
              Don't write it down, don't give the dark powers the right to
              say: "Such souls are better off drowned; the world has been
              cleansed."

MANDARIN   *(With fear.)*
              Drowned? Drowned? Will we drown?
              (Jumps up.)
              My children!

MAGICIAN   *(Pulls him down.)*
              Don't shout; a wise man doesn't shout; he knows the loudest
              cry is silence, and he falls silent.

MANDARIN   I *will* shout! We must run to the hills, climb the trees, save
              ourselves!

MAGICIAN   *(Laughs.)*
              Save ourselves?
              *(The Mandarin is about to reply but the Magician comes and
              puts his hand over his mouth.)*
              Shut that mouth of yours, that large, shameless wound.

MANDARIN   May you be cursed! You tear down the boundaries that
              separate man from the demon; you break the sacred chain

that holds the brain inside the head of man.
Cut out his tongue Buddha, gouge out his eyes!

MAGICIAN   Don't worry, if Buddha could, he would have gouged out my
eyes long ago, for I have learned his secret. I saw! I saw! I
saw!
We both conquered hope, we conquered fear; I, too, am a
king, like Buddha, a king of Nothingness; and I wear a
royal crown
Of black air!

MEN   Be quiet! Be still! The women open their arms; be still, so
Buddha,
The Great Lover, may hear them.

FIRST WOMAN   Buddha, Buddha, I renounce Mei-Ling, the cursed sister of
Chiang. I renounce Mei-Ling.
I heard nothing; she told me nothing; I never spoke to her!

SECOND WOMAN   I, too, empty my heart before you, grandfather; I wash it
again and again. I will lock myself in my house. I will yoke
myself to the holy submission of daughter, wife and
mother.
A slave, a happy slave, with three sacred, beloved chains —
one is called Father, the other Husband, the third Son.
And I will again cram my foot inside the iron mold.

THIRD WOMAN   A curse on schools and letters; a curse on ships that go to
foreign shores!
A curse on eyes that gaze beyond China!

FIRST WOMAN   Buddha, look, we bring you a bowl of milk, so you may
remember your mother, the milk that suckled you, so you
may take pity on woman.

SECOND WOMAN   Look, we bring you blossoming branches; it's spring, the trees
are swollen, our breasts are swollen; give us time,
grandfather, to kiss, to give birth...

THIRD WOMAN   ...To make our little life immortal.

MAGICIAN   *(To the Mandarin.)*
The trees are swollen, the breasts are swollen, the waters are
swollen.
Poor little souls; they shout, and God is deaf; they cry out to

him, "Lean over and look," but God is blind. They plead,
"Put out your hand, help us," but where will He find hands
and feet and brains, where will He find a heart to pity
mankind. He's
A River, and He descends!

FIRST MAN   O Buddha, Buddha, give orders to your slave, Yangtze. He
moves slowly; he's blind and deaf; he doesn't understand.
Order him not to devour the just and the unjust alike — but
only one.
Do you hear his name? Chiang! Chiang! Chiang! Do you
hear? Chiang! Let him devour *him*, only *him!*

FIRST WOMAN   And his sister, Mei-Ling! And his sister, the accursed
Mei-Ling! Don't forget Mei-Ling, grandfather.
She's to blame for what I've done. She moved heaven and
earth to take me from my home, from my cares, from my
woman's heart!
Buddha, help me!

MAGICIAN   *(To the Mandarin.)*
Wretched men, they don't know...they don't know the great
secret...

MANDARIN   What great secret?

MAGICIAN   Lean over, they must not hear us...Buddha and Yangtze...
Gather your little wits together, old man, or they'll escape
you...

MANDARIN   Buddha and Yangtze?

MAGICIAN   Why are you trembling? Do you understand? Do you
understand the great secret?
Buddha and the Yangtze are one!

FIRST OLD MAN   Eh, Magician, eh, great exorcist! Why do you sit idly by and
talk so sweetly during the greatest danger? All year we feed
you, give you drink, clothe you, for this very moment.
Perform your magic, gather the wind, pound it with the
hammer of your mind, mold it into a sword — and plunge it
into Chiang's neck!

MAGICIAN   *(Weary, softly.)*
Wretched little people, let's help them.

	(He rises, stretches out his hand and approaches Buddha. His lips move, as though murmuring an exorcism.)
FIRST OLD MAN	He's casting the great exorcisms, be quiet! He's calling the spirits, cluck, cluck, cluck — like baby chicks!
FIRST MAN	I hear voices, the clashing of arms, the honing of knives, and horses descending from the air. Horses pass through our brows — and our brows cast off sparks like stones.
SECOND OLD MAN	It's the spirits...the spirits! Be quiet!
MAGICIAN	*(Chants the exorcism and claps his hands as though in invitation, then turns toward the old men.)* Let the old men approach. Come close, don't be afraid. Who among you is the eldest? Which of you has seen the most light, the most darkness, has licked the most honey, drunk the most poison? Let him come forward!
FIRST OLD MAN	I'm the one! Today I'm a hundred years old. I was born on the same day, on the same hour as the rebel's father, the old Master. He, Lying on a velvet-strewn bed, on a downy mattress — and I on the manure in his courtyard. But both of us, praise God, were born naked, were born naked snails. We came naked and we'll leave naked; God is just.
MAGICIAN	Give me your knife. *(The old man takes the knife from his belt and gives it to him. The Magician turns to Buddha, mimics, in dance, the act of murder. Everyone watches silently. Suddenly Buddha slightly bows his head. The crowd falls to the ground in frenzy.)*
PEOPLE	A miracle! A miracle! Buddha moved his head! I saw him! I saw him! I heard him, he said "Yes!"
MAGICIAN	*(Sitting cross-legged, smiles.)* Poor, wretched little people...
MANDARIN	Is this your magic, you mocker of gods? I'll write it down,

I'll denounce you to future generations. I'll say: See with
what lies the famous Magician Hu-Ming tricked the people...

MAGICIAN   *(Laughing)*
             And the gods! The people and the gods! Mark the gods down
             too, penpusher; don't be afraid!

MANDARIN   Good! Good! Good!
             (Writes with passion.)

MAGICIAN   Write, write, penpusher! You think a miracle is some rare
             bird that descends from the sky, a dragon that rises from
             Hell and upsets laws.
             The true miracle, old man, is the heart of man.

MANDARIN   And Buddha, what of Buddha who moved his head?

MAGICIAN   Eh, what can the poor gods do? They've a secret machine
             inside them. After all, we put them together,
             We put them together, I tell you.
             You press a button and they obey. You press lightly, and they
             say no; you press harder, and they say yes.
             The soul grows bitter; it grows bitter on pondering its
             secrets...
             (Beats his chest.)
             Smothering, dark, sly, full of paints and rags and gold
             paper is this workshop...

MUSICIAN   *(Beating the drum wildly.)*
             Oh! Oh! Oh!
             (Chiang's soldiers arrive panting, ragged, wounded.)

FIRST OLD MAN   Eh, eh, gallant lads, who's chasing you? Wait!

FIRST SOLDIER   Rejoice, brothers, we were conquered! The Ancestors have
                 won, the immortal dead arose, shouted,
                 And Chiang's army was scattered!

PEOPLE   The miracle! The miracle! The beginning of salvation!

MANDARIN   Don't shout, your work is finished, but mine is just beginning.
             Come here, you with blood on your chin!
             What's happened? How did it happen? When did it happen?
             Speak clearly, so I can write it down, that you, too, may
             be saved, you poor wretches.

FIRST SOLDIER	Buddha! It was Buddha! Brothers, listen; listen old man, and write. While we were digging the graves in the Monastery...
SECOND SOLDIER	...And laying bare the sacred bones of the Ancestors to burn them...may Chiang be cursed!
THIRD SOLDIER	...Buddha leaped out of the earth...Buddha, my brothers, and he roared.
PEOPLE	And Chiang? Was Chiang killed?
FIRST SOLDIER	Killed? Are demons ever killed? My tongue is dry, I can't... *(Turns to second soldier.)* Comrade, *you* speak!
SECOND SOLDIER	What can I say? We were killed or crippled; we left our noses, our hands, our ears on the fields.
THIRD SOLDIER	We're lost! We're lost! *(To the whores.)* Open your arms, women, comfort us.
WHORES	Come! Come! Come!
FIRST WOMAN	Where is my son? I don't see him.
SECOND SOLDIER	*(Pointing to the ground)* Down there.
SECOND WOMAN	And my husband? Has anyone seen him? Where can he be?
SECOND SOLDIER	*(Pointing to ground)* Down there.
THIRD WOMAN	My three brothers? My nephews?
THIRD SOLDIER	*(Pointing to ground)* Down there! Down there! Down there! Stop crying, women; this is war, it wants to eat; it's a tiger, it doesn't eat grass, It eats men! *(Forcefully opens the window of the Tower. The crowd huddles together, frightened.)*
PEOPLE	See how forcefully he's opened the tower window! Now the Old Man will appear.

Quiet!

MANDARIN   Friends, who will bring him the good news, that his
soul may sweeten? Tell him that his rebel son
was defeated.

PEOPLE   You go...
No, no...you!
He'll pour boiling water on us again from the battlements.

MAGICIAN   Li-Li-Foo!

LI-LI-FOO   Command me.

MAGICIAN   Go, beloved, knock and shout: "Master, your son Chiang has
been defeated!"

LI-LI-FOO   I'm going.
*(The people step back, frightened, and watch Li-Li-Foo
knocking on the Tower door.)*
Master! Master!

MAGICIAN   Louder!

LI-LI-FOO   Master!
(The tower door opens. Li-Li-Foo bows in obeisance.)
Master, your son Chiang has been defeated!

OLD MAN   *(Joyous voice from within)*
Say it again!

LI-LI-FOO   Master, your son Chiang has been defeated!
*(Loud, strong laughter is heard from inside. The music rises
joyously as the Old Man appears. He is holding his ivory staff
of authority. Behind him Old Koag holds the Old Man's
sword across his outstretched arms. As the Old Man crosses
the threshold, the two lanterns, as huge as urns, light up on
each side of the door. Behind the Old Man follows Young
Chiang's wife. The people and the soldiers prostrate
themselves.)*

MAGICIAN   *(To the Mandarin.)*
Look at his right hand; it drips blood.

MANDARIN   Blood? Blood? I see nothing.

MAGICIAN   Tomorrow, you'll see.

(*The Old Man remains silent, walking slowly among the prostrated crowd, toward Buddha.*)

MANDARIN (*To the Magician.*)
Li-Liang, the wife of Chiang! Look, her lips smile,
But her eyes are filled with tears.

MAGICIAN The miracle! This is the miracle of woman. Patience, virtue, sweetness. Her heart breaks...but she smiles. She bows her head...but her body rises to twice its height.
She remains silent...but her silence rips mountains apart. She sees the man she loves dying...but she takes him quietly by the hand,
And leaves with him.

MANDARIN (*With fear.*)
Who's dying? Who's leaving? What are you ranting about?

PEOPLE Quiet! Be still! The Nobleman has spread out his arms and prays.

OLD MAN The Nobleman carries cities and villages on his shoulders and reports to Buddha every night before sleeping.
The Nobleman thinks of farms — seeds, crops, sun, rain —
And the fields turn green...He thinks of sheep, oxen, mares — and fields and mountains bleat, moo and whinny.
He thinks of mankind — and cradles overflow with babies, fireplaces crackle...
All joys, all disasters are his; if the river swells, it's his fault; if the crops rot, it's the Nobleman's fault.
It's my fault that my son, that cursed rebel, raised a hand against you, O Buddha, but I refused to eat or drink or sleep for three days and nights. I cast spells against the dark, invisible forces — and see, I've struck him down!
(*Strikes the ground with his staff.*)
Ancestors, eh, Ancestors! The ground swells, the dead rise...
(*Listens.*)
What did you say, grandfather? I can't hear.
(*To the people.*)
Quiet! Be quiet! The Ancestors are speaking!
Yes, yes, his army has been conquered and scattered, the earth has finally returned to its eternal rounds. Rise out of the earth; the rain has stopped, twilight is falling, no one

38

will see you. Sit to my left and right, the festival is
beginning. O, both dead and living, there's a great joy, a
double joy to be celebrated tonight:
The rebel has been defeated, and Buddha has been set free
into the air!
*(Li-Liang holds back her sobs with difficulty. The Old Man
turns and places his hand tenderly on her shoulder.)*
Li-Liang, beloved wife of my stubborn son...
(Strokes her hair, turns to the crowd.)
Every virtue has two heads: one is all light, the other all
darkness. War, too, has two faces: the one is called Peace.
Peace has two faces: the other is called War.
You can see only the one, but I see both, because I am your
Nobleman. That is the meaning of Nobleman.
(Sighs.)
Life is heavy, the heart two-sided, and I don't know what I
want...
(Raises his hands to Buddha.)
O Lord, dreadful spirit, dark mouth, you speak and I don't
hear; my head is a deep cave filled with bears and haunted
honeycombs.
Untamed powers, gentle powers, inhabit my breast and
quarrel. Buddha, great thought, make them friends.
I bow, look rapaciously at earth and say: "It's mine!" But
immediately I quiet down, the honeycomb melts and drips
inside me — and I divide the earth among men.
I look at man and want to kill him. Why? I don't know. I
want to. I look at woman, my eyes blur and I want to
sleep with her. I look at my son,
The blood rises to my eyes, and I shout: "Cursed is the seed
of man!"
My virtue is a pure-white lily that sprouts out of fertile layers
of dishonor, then swiftly withers; to the right and left of
me are the dark forces of madness, and my heart struggles
to keep its balance as it labors to cross, with fear and
trembling, the thin bridge of a hair.
Through how many thousands of years, through how many
thousands of bodies must I still pass, O Lord, to throw off
my burdens? That my flesh may become spirit — and the
spirit, air?
O Buddha, you have cast off your burdens, you have emptied

39

and cleansed your heart, your loins, your liver, your
bladder, your phallus — you have escaped.
Help me to escape too!
That is why I restrain myself from killing. That is why I sit
quietly in my Tower and smoke hashish and sail like a
cloud in the wind...
And that is why each year, today, on your day of festival, I
celebrate your liberation — that you may remember me,
too, Buddha, and liberate me.
I light the huge lanterns, send invitations, slaughter oxen,
distribute wine and hashish generously, that the people
may be happy, and then bring the renowned Magician
from his Monastery
To place wings on Necessity that it may fly!

MAGICIAN   *(To the Mandarin.)*
Look, look at him — how green he's become, how swollen, like
a drum...he's floating on his back over his Tower...
And holding a baby in his arms.

MANDARIN   What did he do? What's happened to him? I can't hear...

MAGICIAN   He's been liberated!

OLD MAN   Raise your eyes and see, Buddha: It's for you I call the
renowned Magician to cast his spells, to turn the wheel, to
bring the future before us,
To give flesh, bones and a voice to man's hopes.
(Claps his hands.)
Eh, Hu-Ming!

MAGICIAN   *(Rises, approaches.)*
I stand before you, Noble One. Command me.

OLD MAN   Life's a heavy burden, Hu-Ming, lighten it; place wings on our
shoulders so we may escape. Take the screwdriver and
unscrew our temples so our minds may widen, so we may
see. Are you ready?

MAGICIAN   I was never more ready, O Noble One, than I am tonight.
Buddha never blew upon me so strongly, never has he been
so weighed down with heavy, intoxicating aromas as he is
tonight. Command me!

OLD MAN   Put us to sleep that we may dream; or if we are sleeping now

40

perhaps, nudge us that we may waken.

Call the spirits, open the five doors of the senses, turn life into
    a fairy tale.

(To the two slaves.)

Bring the large censors to dispel the stench of man, that the
    spirits may come. And place stools to the right and left of
    me for the Ancestors,

And you, beloved Li-Liang, come, sit beside me, to see the
    truth and be unburdened. The world is a cloud, Li-Liang,
    a little cloud;

Sit down and let's watch it scatter…Don't cry, please,
    Li-Liang, mother of my one dear grandson, don't cry, for
    if your milk turns sour and my grandson becomes ill, then

The world will end.

MAGICIAN   *(He prays first before Buddha, then before the Nobleman, and
finally before the People. With the long blue feather he holds,
he lightly traces a magic circle.)*

I bring down from the sky and carve on the earth the magic
    circle with its twelve signs of the zodiac;

I open an arena where the great athletes, the characters of my
    fantasy, may enter and fight.

No one must step inside the holy circle!

*(The people step back and sit down cross-legged. Slaves enter;
they light censors, and perfume the surroundings. The
Magician nails twelve multi-colored figures around the circle,
murmuring.)*

I nail on earth the twelve mystic beasts that the sun, the
    Buddha of the sky, carries with him on his rounds: The
    Cock, the Hare, the Tiger, the Ape, the Pig, the Snake,
    the Ox, the Dragon, the Dog, the Sheep, the Rat, the
    Horse.

*(Slaves bring two chairs on which the Old Man and Li-Liang
sit. Stools are placed to the right and left for the Ancestors.
The slaves light the Old Man's pipe. He smokes and closes
his eyes in bliss. A sweet seductive music begins. Slaves bring
the people narghiles, who smoke hashish and also close their
eyes in serenity. For a while nothing is heard but the music.
The Old Man opens his eyes.)*

OLD MAN   Eh, Hu-Ming, hurry, call out to the Hopes, those great nurses

41

of man. Call out to the Hopes to come, to give us their
breasts.
(He closes his eyes again. The Magician puts on a round,
yellow mask. Music. Silently the set crumbles, as in a dream.
The scenery changes—the Yangtze encircles all like a ring.
In the center is an island, and in its center a huge, dried-out
tree. Underneath the tree, sitting cross-legged, is Buddha.)

MAGICIAN   I place the yellow mask of the Spirit on my face. Descend,
horrid bird of prey, and eat.
O creations of earth, water and air, open your eyes, open
your ears—enter into your liberation.

PEOPLE   Oh I see a holy vision, I see old grandfather River descending
quietly, quietly, quietly.
I see an enormous tree rising without leaves or flowers or
fruit.
Brothers, we've anchored on a desert island. It has darkened
and an invisible lion roars in the darkness.
It must be the Spirit; it's not a lion, it must be the Spirit. Be
quiet!

MAGICIAN   Don't shout; Buddha stirs in the darkness; his beloved disciple
Mogalana has fallen at his feet—be quiet so we may hear
what they're saying.

BUDDHA   Mogalana!

MOGALANA   Here I am, Lord, command me!

BUDDHA   Mogalana!

MOGALANA   I'm at your feet, Father, lower your eyes to see me.
I heard your voice as I was descending the stairs of the
monastery, bathed and wrapped in my yellow robe,
holding the beggar-bowl in my hand. And like the eagle
that grabs a lamb and lifts it to the clouds, and then
suddenly plunges down and casts it into its nest,
So did your mind seize me and fling me at your feet, O Lord.
Command me!

BUDDHA   Mogalana, dextrous and compassionate disciple, cast your
eyes along the banks of the river; those are not ants you
see, they are not grasshoppers, they are not waterworms,
They are people! Do you pity them?

42

MOGALANA   Forgive me, Lord, I do pity them; I've not yet been able, with
            great thoughts and constant fasting, to transform my heart
            and turn it into spirit.
            A piece of flesh cries inside my breast, a piece of fat, a piece
            of man. A Cry. Forgive me, O king of air!
            I know well, O Merciless Thought, that all these, all souls
            and bodies, are but phantoms of the mind, of the invisible
            fakir who plays. I said:
            "I shall sit cross-legged and will not rise until I empty out my
            entrails." I said:
            "Reject your eyes, Mogalana, reject your ears, your nose,
            your tongue, your touch, even compassion; reject the
            creations you see; they do not exist. Reject the weeping
            you hear; it does not exist. Reject the perfumes and stench,
            reject water, milk and bread; stretch out your hand and
            choke your heart.
            Reject good and evil, freedom and force, gods and animals;
            they do not exist. Blow upon the lantern of the mind and
            put it out, that the world may be extinguished with it."
            I shouted, I shouted in the desert, but I could not tear down
            my chest, Father.
            And a little while ago as I was descending the stairs of the
            Monastery, I thought of mankind, and my eyes blurred.
            Forgive me, Father, I cannot as yet turn my heart into air.

BUDDHA   Mogalana, steady your flesh, descend, step on earth, appear
            before the people. Raise the Great Seed you hold,
            Mogalana, and cast it.

MOGALANA   What Seed, Father?

BUDDHA   The Buddha. Run, Mogalana, and toss it into the earthen
            furrows of their minds. Help it take root inside them, to
            blossom and bear fruit that their entrails may eat.
            With patience, with sweetness, Mogalana, unleash into their
            minds the final, triumphant march.
            The Liberator has risen, he has risen to help them, and like an
            elephant has turned his head slowly and bid the world
            farewell...
            Open, Mogalana, unleash your mind like the deep river, bring
            down mud, trees, scorpions, gods, ideas — drown the world
            with your brain, Mogalana.

43

Pity the world, Mogalana, uproot the houses of men, set them sailing upon the sea of imagination, crush them like boats, crush them that they may be saved!

Stretch out your hand to the wind, Mogalana, turn back the wheel of earth —

Let Buddha die again.

PEOPLE   It's Mogalana, brothers, the dreadful disciple of Buddha! He swings his right hand joyously in wide circles — as though he's sowing seed.

I'm afraid. He turns his face upon us slowly.

Like a moon eaten up by darkness, like a moon suddenly appearing from behind a mountain and hanging above the ravines — look, it's his head!

Open your mouth, Mogalana! I can see mountains in your eyes and a large flock of yellow birds,

And a large turtle dove in front with a huge neck leading the way.

MOGALANA   He's coming, he's coming; he's descending the mountains, passing over the waters as he shines in his saffron robe like the sun, and holding his beggar-bowl upside-down;

He doesn't want to eat anymore, he's had his fill of food and drink.

He's coming, he's coming; bare your shoulders and worship him, the fully Awakened One is coming!

As pure white as the light, he set out with his mind loaded with great ideas, his hands loaded with deeds; he crossed through forests and mountains, over gods and thoughts; he passed through the whole ravine of futility, bidding the world farewell slowly, lingeringly.

The Perfect One is looking on all things as though for the first time. The Perfect One is looking on all things as though for the last time; and see, soon he will arrive beneath this tree where he was born,

To lie down, blow on himself and vanish,

In a village, when sickness struck him severely, then Buddha, the Lord of life and death, swallowed a piece of meat, like a grain of wheat,

But his soul would not accept it, and Death appeared.

Death stood before him and uncovered his own shoulder with terror to worship him, but the great athlete raised his

44

impregnable head encircled with towers and airy
battle-ments, smiled and said to the Mind:
"Take up your sword, don't let anyone approach. Who is this
slave who stands before me and bares his shoulder to
worship me? Don't let him approach.
I want to reach the tree where I was born; with my knees
locked to my chin, holding the much-travelled soles of my
feet in my hands, and rolled up into a round ball the way
I was once crammed into a small womb, I want to return
to that large womb, the earth."
He spoke, and the Mind raised its sword, and Death stepped
back in seven large strides, like a slave, and waited for
Buddha to command.
The Master rose from the ground, and then, without haste,
holding out his empty and yet sated beggar's bowl, he
started out again.
The days and nights moved with him like white and black
birds — and he went on ahead, leading the way.
He bent over the rim of every well and blessed the waters;
and at once the waters relaxed and smiled serenely,
brightly, like the eye of Buddha.
He stood at every lookout and sang in a quiet, calm voice
as though casting magic spells on invisible forces, as
though he were a shepherd calling out to his sheep...
The great Traveler went on and on. Like a king after a great
war, he was returning to his capitol — to Death.
A few days ago, at noon, he stood beneath a silver-branched,
bare fig tree, touched a bough and shook it slowly,
cordially, like the hand of a friend. For a long while he
remained silent, and then, turning to Ananta, his beloved
disciple, he spoke softly and instructed him:
"Beneath this fig tree, Ananta, Temptation slid one noon and
found me. I was hungry, and he held a bowl of rice in his
hand; I was thirsty, and he held a jug of refreshing water
on his shoulder. I hadn't touched a woman in seven years,
and now a girl I had once longed for in dream, when my
soul was still asleep,
Slithered toward me full of desire, her breasts naked.
But I embraced the barren, bone-dry fig tree, and all at once,
Ananta, my hunger was filled, my thirst was quenched, as
though I had eaten a basket of cool, honeyed figs;

45

I became serene, as though I had embraced a woman, and
Temptation laughed and vanished.
Ananta, the holy fig tree is also laden with visions like
honeyed figs, is laden with deeds. This is my command:
Commemorate this tree.
It, too, stood by my side in battle."
He climbed, he climbed the rocky slopes, he climbed and his
memory increased — at times he thought of a green lizard
that once upon a time used to sit on this rock and sun
itself;
At times he thought of an apple that, once upon a time, hung
from a tall branch at noon and smelled sweetly;
And at times he thought of an idea which, as once he had
climbed up this high mountain peak, plunged down upon
him like an eagle and dug its nails into his head.
He went on and on...Behind him followed the days and the
nights, behind him his disciples, behind him the sky and
the stars — together they all followed the holy traces of his
feet.
And at night, when we had washed our earthen bowls, when
we had washed our hands and mouths, we sat cross-legged
around him — and then with upturned hands that glowed in
the moonlight the Teacher began to speak in the night —
And as he spoke, the honeysuckle blossomed above him, the
sky blossomed above him like a garden, and on earth
insects, dogs and foxes crawled on their bellies behind the
disciples and struck up a dance of their own,
All ears, silence and obedience.
The sweat ran from our armpits, our backs undulated like
waters when sharks glide beneath the surface, our minds
crossed the bridge of hair above the abyss of madness;
And there, with his towering, unsweating brow encircled by
night-butterflies, and glowing like phosphorus in the
darkness;
There, looking straight ahead, neither up at the sky nor down
at the earth but lightly, straight ahead at the height of man,
with slim, sharp fingers, signifying his thought,
There sat Buddha, smiling
But yesterday at dusk, before the stone hut of an old
shepherd, the pale Teacher stopped and said, "I'm tired."
Greatly agitated, the trembling disciples surrounded and

supported him…Ananta spread out the lion skin his father,
the King, had given him to sleep on,

And Buddha sat on it cross-legged, holding his head high,
bright and motionless — like a flame in a blue and windless
night…

He turned his gaze to the North, toward the graves of the
Ancestors — and there, from the sky's foundations a thick,
blue-black cloud appeared, like a crow descending,
widening, filling the sky, and approaching…

"It's Death! Death!" But the Master smiled,

Closed his eyes and slept, and seven stars above him like
swords kept guard. And the disciples, like honey-bees that
encircle the Queen Bee for fear of losing her, clung and
clustered about him mournfully,

And I, lying low beside him, watched in the starlight two
mystic wheels shining under the soles of his feet.

I watched the sky turning like a wheel, the stars marching all
together toward the West, and the North Star, too,

— In which sea-warriors and mule-drivers trust as certain and
unmoving —

I watched it also moving toward the West…

I jumped up. Compassion for mankind cut through me deeply
as I strode over the sleeping swarm, made the rounds of the
villages at midnight, beating on the doors and shouting:

"Come! Come! Come! The Liberator is striding over the earth,
he's striding over life, desire and fear — and he's coming to
lie down under the holy Tree where he was born, to gather
his strength and scatter in the wind!"

Compassion cut through me for the animals also, for the
birds and the worms: "Brother beasts, birds, worms," I
shouted, "Come, Buddha, the Great Brother, is crossing
the forests, the mountains and the waters on his way to
die. Come, all of you,

Let's all plunge into his tranquil eye, before it closes!"

A groaning arose from the caves; the earth broke open as the
worms appeared; the wind shone like the head of a great
leader from the red, yellow and blue feathers descending…

I pitied the gods, too; I raised my arms to the sky and
shouted: "Gods, O all-powerful phantoms of man's head,
mount the clouds, roll down the rainbow, emerge from
under the brainless minds of man, come, come!

47

Buddha has stretched out his hand, he's thrust back the bolt, he's opened the door of freedom! Latch onto his saffron robe, O gods,
And free yourselves with him!"

PEOPLE   Brothers, Mogalana has stopped speaking. He wipes away his sweat, he's smiling...
He smiles, and a fire licks his lips, rolls down his neck, his chest, his thighs, his feet — and spills over the earth.

BLOSSOMING
CHERRY TREE   (Bursts into wails.)
Ah, ah, I didn't know that Buddha lurks in ambush behind the kiss.
O flesh, we are lost! Koag, don't touch me!

YOUNG KOAG   O Blossoming Cherry Tree, I didn't know that the kiss lurks in ambush behind Buddha. Forgive me! Let me touch your lips for a lightning moment before they rot!
Quiet! Quiet! Mogalana is opening his mouth again!

MOGALANA   My brethren, join hands in a hopeless, happy dance around the Holy Tree!
I dance, I clap my hands, I raise my neck and shout. But I don't shout — I sing.
Sing, also, beloved shadows, sing with me.

ALL TOGETHER   (Singing.)

Like the gold silkworm, Buddha has moored
On the branch of flowerless silence.
He's eaten all the leaves,
He's eaten all the leaves of the mulberry tree,
He's eaten all the leaves
And turned them into silk.
He doesn't want to eat anymore, or smell, or touch...
His bowels have emptied, his heart has lightened,
He's become all mind and air in the wilderness,
He's become mind and air
And is lightly scattered.

(A heavy sigh is heard. Mogalana stops the song.)

MOGALANA   Who sighed? I feel a human breast resisting...Open up, make way...who sighed?

48

YOUNG MAN   A young man. A free spirit that rises above the abyss of
                    liberation and speaks his mind...
                 Mogalana, you've never
                 Loved woman, and life seems to you like smoke that weaves
                    and unweaves, becomes a city, a cloud, a woman, an idea,
                    and that climbs and disappears
                 Over the flaming desert of your mind...
                 With what right, Mogalana, do you speak and judge? What
                    can he know about the spirit who has not loved the flesh?
                 It's your life, Mogalana, that's but shadow and smoke,
                    because you've loved only ideas that play, intertwining in
                    air and disappearing — and they have no poisoning voice,
                    they have no lips for you to kiss,
                 They have no body for you to grasp tightly in the hour of
                    the great separation and to feel it in your arms, between
                    your legs, quivering and warm
                 As it escapes you.

MOGALANA   O human breast, O warm, tortured flesh! This flesh suffers
                    so much, my brothers, that it turns into spirit...Be silent
                    that we may hear.

YOUNG MAN   Ascetic Mogalana, the earth is real, the spirit is real, the body
                    of man is real, all flesh and tears, because one woman
                    became for me, as your own teacher says,
                 A murderess, a thief, a mother, a mistress, a sister, a wife
                    and a slave.
                 She killed me every midnight, Mogalana, when we lay down
                    together to sleep; she fought, pale and mute; froth rimmed
                    her clenched teeth as she hissed and entwined her body
                    around my thighs;
                 And she snatched whatever these worker's hands of mine
                    earned, Mogalana, and adorned her lovely head like a
                    gaudy ornament...
                 And at other times she took me to her breast and cradled
                    me and struggled to thrust me inside her flesh, bearing
                    me like a son...
                 And at other times again, at dawn, she laughed and shook
                    me by the shoulders. We'd wake in the high rosy
                    mountain air; we'd stride joyously, one beside the other,
                    beating our staffs and our thick wooden clogs on the
                    stones...

49

And when I became ill, she stayed awake all night by my
   pillow, like a sister, and we talked about our lives as
   children, about the rain, about the fields, about our parents.
And my chest breathed quietly, resting beside the small
   breast of my sister.
And when, dressed in my rough working clothes I leaped up
   and bounded across the threshold, as the dog went
   ahead, barking, with raised tail, and the waddling cattle
   straggled behind, then the two of us set out for the
   fields with our work-tools over our shoulders, harnessed
   to the holy day's work,
And I would turn to look at her, and as wheat bread
   comforts our entrails, so was I comforted.
And when I returned, as the lanterns were lit, and sat in our
   courtyard, Mogalana, she knelt like a slave and with
   refreshing water soothed my flaming feet and my knees;
   she lit the lamp, Mogalana, above the fireplace, she
   moved inside the house like a pure spirit and spread our
   humble meal in the yard under the grape arbor...
And I sat, Mogalana, motionless, with half-closed eyelids
   and admired her — and I trembled lest it was a dream,
   lest my beloved full-bodied woman disappear and scatter
   in the wind...
And one morning, barefooted, sheathed in his saffron robe,
   stretching out his beggar's bowl, Buddha came and leaned
   against my door-post.
My wife went out to the courtyard and was terrified to see a
   column of fire swirling at the threshold, passing beyond
   the rooftop, setting fire to the neighborhood.
And as she screamed, the fire subsided, and a lion then
   stood in my courtyard and looked at my home calmly,
   innocently — like its landlord.
Then the beast faded in the glittery air, and my wife was
   startled to see a lean figure, eaten away by fasting and
   the rain, by the sun and the mind,
Standing silently at the threshold, smiling at her.
   Thunderstruck by such magic, my wife fell at your
   teacher's feet, weeping and shouting: "Take me!
Take me, for my house can no longer hold me, words and
   deeds can no longer contain me; I'm in despair, take me!
   I shall stand by your side, Master, to cool you with a fan

of peacock feathers."

And when I returned at night, Mogalana, it was the first time
    I had not seen my wife running from the threshold to take
    the work-tools from my shoulder and to lighten my load —
    the door of my house was open, the bed empty, the
    hearth darkened...

Then the neighboring women came, told me everything, and
    I fell to the ground weeping, beating my head against
    the stones, cursing your Teacher...A curse,

A curse on the souls who never knew the bitterness, the
    sweetness, the warmth of a woman and yet judge the
    world! A curse on your Teacher!

MOGALANA   Blaspheme, my brother, blaspheme. Hatred, anger, evil
    words and blasphemy are all a sickness in us — spit them
    out, brother, spit them out and be cleansed.

You have reached the summit of pain; liberation begins
    from the summit of pain...My brother, what was your
    wife's name?

YOUNG MAN   Moudita.

MOGALANA   Moudita! My brother, like a wild palm tree in the scorching
    sun, with a long fan of peacock feathers, your wife
    stands erect by the side of the Liberator

And fans and cools Buddha.

YOUNG MAN   I'll grab her by the hair and bring her back home!

MOGALANA   What hair, my brother? You'll see but a phantom fanning
    Buddha...a phantom, and it wears a saffron robe, its hair
    is cut to the roots, its breasts have sagged, its ribs glow
    from holiness and fasting...

It's not a phantom, it's your wife; it's not a crazed bitch,
    it's not a dry bamboo reed, it's not a tumble-down shack
    — it's your wife.

Awaken, brother, awaken, brothers, toss your heads, free
    your bodies from the yoke of life, liberate yourselves from
    the threshing and winnowing, set your cattle free.

The fields of Buddha are made of green air, his yoke is a
    blue shadow, and his ox-goad

Is a tall, compassionate thought.

PEOPLE   Mogalana leans on the Holy Tree, and all the branches
           shake and intertwine like arms.
           A shrill cry, like that of a new born babe's rises from the
           roots...
           My knees buckle with fear, brothers. Over our heads,
           desperate, serene, pure saffron, like a tree in autumn,
           Rises the Spirit!

MOGALANA   Brothers, don't shout; it's the Holy Tree under whose shade
           the Liberator was born, and the sweet cry of the babe
           you hear is his voice.
           One day at dawn, as the Liberator's mother, Maya, was
           strolling slowly by, pale and heavy with child, she spied
           this Tree in full bloom; and as she stood on tiptoe to cut
           a flowering branch,
           Her body creaked like a Palace that opens its golden doors
           for the King to pass. Then labor pains seized her, and
           before her maids could even support her,
           The infant dropped upon the blossoms like a burning coal.
           The earth glowed, and all the gods leaned from the heavens
           to see the small, plump soles of the baby's feet — and
           they were terrified, for on them, like two roses in full
           bloom, flashed
           The two wheels of the law.

PEOPLE   Ah, each leaf of the tree is a people crying out!
           And the ripe, honeyed fruit at the top is Buddha!
           The whole tree rejoices to its roots because it dreams it
           does not exist.

MUSICIANS *(Playing a wild, fast tune and shouting with terror.)*
           Oh! Oh! Oh!

PEOPLE   Who is this gnome of the forest, full of hair, leaves and soil?
           He holds a goad made of a bull's horn, as behind him,
           bleating, groaning, neighing, meowing, follow the tame
           animals, the wild beasts and the insects.
           Brothers, the air is polluted, it stinks like a he-goat in heat.
           What is this thing, my brothers?
           It's no longer a beast, it's not yet human — it must be one of
           the old, great Grandfathers. Be quiet!

MOGALANA   Be quiet! It's the Husband of Earth, that greasy Grandfather
           with his exhausted loins, old man Markalo!

MARKALO   Eh, cunning ascetic with your saffron robe:
           Where are we going? Why are we shouting? Why are we
               weeping? What is that yellow bird that disrupts the air?
           I feel my shoulders shaken by beasts, I see the hills staggering
               under the feet of goats, sheep, bears and rabbits in a rush
               downward —
           They climb up my shoulders and my neck; snails, crabs,
               scorpions and lizards seek shelter on my huge head; turtles
               boom on their hollow shells and run; birds begin to wail;
               that deathbird, the owl, leads the way and all the feathered
               retinue bursts into threnody and sets out.
           Why? Where? I stretch out my neck, I ask, I shout. "Why?
               Why? Where are they going? Where?"

MOGALANA   Welcome to lascivious Markalo, welcome to that great, holy
               martyr, the Scarab, welcome to the dark, heavy loins of
               the Mind, that shameless He-goat,
           You adorn and arm yourself with feathers and horns, you
               gasp, you stick out your gossiping tongue, you shout:
               "Why? Why? Where are we going?"
           Fall down and worship the earth; wait and you shall hear.

PEOPLE   The air and earth have filled the night with horns and wings.
           A huge cicada has hooked on to the Holy Tree and is sawing
               the wind.
           The great Ascetic has seized him, placed him on his palm and
               welcomes him.

MOGALANA   Welcome cicada with your translucent steel wings, with three
               drops of blood on your forehead, with your breast over-
               brimming with song.
           Hook unto the Tree of Death, pierce it, that it may gush with
               honey, that you may eat and become satiated. You're not
               one to live on air and the sky's dew; your insides need
               solid food
           To sing.
           Pierce the black bark of the Tree, pass through the shield of
               earth, touch its warm, soft heart, like the heart of man.
           Sing! Hurry, brother, hurry, there's no time! The green
               locust will arrive at midnight; it will come and we won't
               know it, because it will resemble the spring leaves of trees;
               it will come

53

And it will mow down our slim, singing throat, like grass.
If only we had time to sing but one song, one quick tune, to
   utter one shrill cry, flying hurriedly from one branch to
   another in the night.

PEOPLE   The cicada leaps, buries itself in Mogalana's hair, and begins
              to sing.
           The great Ascetic bends down and welcomes the animals, the
              beasts, the insects.

MOGALANA   Welcome, welcome, welcome to all the Saints!
           Under the stones and waters, under the green trees, some of
              you hermits, others in couples, others in herds, pummel
           The earth, the water, the wind. You eat the dead and the
              living, until the mystic elaboration begins, the invisible
              changes into the visible, the certain to the uncertain, the
              fruit to seed, and you labor to dissolve the breast of earth
              entirely
           And turn it into Spirit.
           Every small insect is a small intact Buddha — a small, intact
              Buddha that thrusts into the earth and works at liberation
              night and day.

MUSICIANS (Playing softly, sweetly, joyfully.)
           Oooh!...

PEOPLE   I hear voices, I see flames shooting from the sky to the earth.
           It's the spirits!
           The spirits, the spirits descending with their multi-colored
              wings!
           A red hawk has clutched the top of my head like a flame! I'm
              on fire!

MOGALANA   The mustering of the Bodiless begins. Make room, men and
              beasts, the spirits are forming and approaching in herds at
              the edge of my eyes.
           A thousand times welcome, spirits of the water, of silence, of
              the wilderness.
           The riverbanks have filled with wooden clogs, stones glitter
              from snow-ankled feet, reeds shout like throats — the time
              has come again for legends to walk the street like men.
           Make way, step back; I've seen the holy birds of the mind,
              the parrots, setting fire to the wind with their golden
              plumes.

54

My brothers, I hear that Saripoutta, the greatest disciple of
all, is plowing the earth with his holy ox-cart, sinking into
the soil the four heavy, cypress-wood
Wheels of the law.
Saripoutta! Saripoutta! Great rivers separated us, mountains
and years stood between us. He sowed the Word to the
right, and I sowed it on the other bank, to the left. I went
on
Alone and raging, shouting in the wilderness. He, I hear,
roamed the inhabited world in an ox-cart with women,
dancers, ascetics and monkeys. He entered large cities,
pitched his tent at bazaars, and crowds gathered about
him, laughed at him, goaded him, pelted him with stones.
And he, quiet, smiling and motionless, with the strength of
his mind alone in the empty light, wound, rewound and
wound again the youth, the flight, the passions and the
liberation of Buddha.
At once the cities filled with saffron robes, hearts grew
calm again, brains behind walled brows blossomed like
jasmine and scented the air —
And Saripoutta yoked the ox-cart again, marshalled and
gathered his holy army inside himself again, and all
together, laughing, playing and whistling, they all set out
to
sow liberation further still.
And as loyal shepherd boys rove around their flocks, going
at times to the front with the shepherd like his foster sons,
at times spreading out to the sides and the tail-end of the
flock, to keep it together lest it scatter,
So, I hear, do parrots like dogs of the wind follow
Saripoutta's divine flock, and at times sit on the oxen's
horns and mock the people, at times sit on Saripoutta's
right shoulder
And mock the mighty gods.
And as they approach the cities, these intelligent birds scatter,
scamper up the eaves of the houses, hang from the
windows, hold onto the women's skirts and shout like
heralds
Of a caravan great in words, proverbs and fantasies: "Come!
Come! Come!"

PEOPLE   Oh, red, yellow and green birds fill the air with their wings.

The herald has arrived, dressed in parrot feathers; he stands
under the Holy Tree and shouts.
What is he shouting? Quiet, so we can hear!

HERALD   (Dressed like a parrot.)
Come! Come! Come! Saripoutta has arrived in his ox-cart,
Saripoutta is here with his miracle-working fakirs,
Saripoutta has arrived with his trained gods and monkeys,
with a great variety of bodies and demons!
Wash your feet, rub your beards and your hair with heavy
aromas, paint your fists and the soles of your feet, raise
your hands high — the sun has set, the moon rises, the mind
rises from skulls like the moon,
Saripoutta with his holy ox-cart stands before you.

PEOPLE   Oh, is this a spirit, a man, a bird, or a gigantic yellow
feather that leaps from the steering wheel of the ox-cart and
touches the ground?
It's not a bird, it's not a feather, it's not a spirit, it's not a
man. It's Saripoutta,
Saripoutta, brothers, who treads on earth and opens his arms.
The two great disciples embrace. They touch cheek with
cheek, motionless, speechless...They cry and laugh and
caress each other, slowly, emotionally,
Like wild doves in a weed-grown monastery courtyard.
Quiet! The Two Great Masters are speaking!

MOGALANA Brother, there's nothing left of you for me to clutch. See how
the Great Thought has eaten up all your flesh! Only your
throat remains to laugh with.
Only your brow stands like a tower over a vanished city.

SARIPOUTTA You hold the Spirit firmly, brother, lest it eat you. I marvel
at you, touch your shoulders, and my hands are contented
as though I had lain them
On the shiny rumps of a bull.
I lean my head on your chest — and I hear a sea beating and
laboring, I hear people shouting, rivers descending,
The Spirit blowing over cities like a great fire, like a great
sickness, destroying streets. A thousand times welcome!

MOGALANA My joy is so sweet and holy at seeing you, my brother, that I
can't conquer it.

56

Ah, what is this earth, with what harmonious entanglement
do shadows skillfully embrace and nestle in the heart of
man
And no longer want to leave the body.
I hold you like a holy toy at dawn, filled with light and
meaning.

PEOPLE   These two famous disciples seem to me like two great rivers
that have watered villages and cities, that have raised
numberless generations of men, numberless generations of
fishes, numberless generations of reeds, and now suddenly,
at the bend of an enormous mountain,
They merge, foam, dance and become one.

MOGALANA   Just as the beetle carries the yellow pollen of flowers on his
feet and wings, on his horns and belly, and goes leaping
across the gardens,
So do you, brother, pass by in your saffron robe, mounting
the earth with your ox-cart.
You pity the people; they battle, but are unable to see great
thoughts in the air — and you pity them and give a simple
and gaudy form to the invisible. Your mind gives birth and
then is dismembered and sits on the temples and breasts of
men.
Animals talk, waters shout, fakirs scramble up the air on
invisible ladders, ideas dance like women, gods climb down
chewing like monkeys.
Men see, hear, smell, taste and touch the great theories.
Your holy ox-cart seems to me like an animal, brother, the
way it groans and climbs the mountains at noonday;
And at night — the way it shines with multi-colored lighted
lanterns surrounding it and walks slowly through the
sleeping plain —
It seems to me like a bright constellation on the dark throat of
night.

SARIPOUTTA   It's not an animal, my brother, it's not a constellation on the
dark throat of night. It's Buddha, my brother Mogalana;
this ox-cart is Buddha, armored well with cypress wood,
irons and sheepskins.
And his head is filled with dancers, ascetics and monkeys.
It's Buddha, and he's coming — the young man with the black,

57

curly hair and the golden sandals.

It's Buddha, and he's coming — the man who has struggled
under the fruitless Tree and after seven years of agony and
struggle has grasped salvation in his fist like a rounded
fruit.

It's Buddha — the old man who has travelled forty years,
burning, enlightening, liberating the world.

It's Buddha, and he's coming like a black swan, serene and
silent, to watch with a lingering glance

His own image dying.

*(The sad song of Blossoming Cherry Tree is heard
softly.)*

BLOSSOMING   *When will this sack, my body, become exhausted,*
CHERRY TREE   *when will the tears that choke me flow away,*
               when will this earth sprout wings and be entrusted,
               o Buddha, to fly away?

*(Slowly the vision dims; the crowd sinks into ecstasy. All
that can be seen is a dark, unmoving lake with a drifting
black swan. Slowly, slowly, this, too, disappears. Music...
but it stops abruptly. Young Chiang appears, angry, dressed
in khaki and holding a whip. A blood-spattered herald
follows him. Chiang watches the people smoking hashish in a
narcotic haze, and he shouts.)*

CHIANG   O heart, disdainful lady, be silent! Be silent, don't become
           angry.

           How many times have I not taken you for a stroll and showed
           you mankind? You followed me like a tiger and wanted to
           pounce upon the passersby. "I don't want them, I don't
           want them," you shouted, "I don't want them!"

           Heart, don't shout; this is what people are, erect swine,
           red-assed monkeys, premature babies, cowards, sickly
           gods — pity them. Don't ask them for virtue, justice,
           nobility — they have none.

           It's better so, it's better! If they did, what need would the
           world have of you, Chiang?

           If they did, what reason would you have to squander your
           life, Chiang, like a nobleman?

           Don't ask for gods as co-workers, my heart; they don't exist.
           It's better so! When they did exist, the gods never deigned

to take us as co-workers; they wanted us for slaves.

They thundered, flashed, flooded the rivers, scattered disease, killed masses of women and children just like that, without reason, to take the wind out of our sails.

Gods, farewell! Have a good trip! I, man, take on the responsibility of the world and sit on the emptied throne.

If I win? Then all the glory is mine. If I lose? Then all the blame is mine — that's what it means to be a nobleman.

I become disgusted, get angry, kill and hate because I love more deeply than others.

I sacrifice my joy, the sweet comforts of my home, my life, all for these blockheads. Why? Who has entrusted you, my heart, with the entire nation? Who gave you such pride or such humility?

Don't ask; forge on, but hold on tightly to the leveling instrument of holy mania.

Chiang, don't forget that you're a man — a man. That is the great title of your nobility.

I'm not God and thus unable to progress further on; I'm a man — and find myself on a journey.

The climb is steep, Chiang, it requires patience, care and stubbornness; it requires love.

Be angry, Chiang, but hold back your anger; be scornful Chiang, but hold back your scorn; love, Chiang, but let no one know it.

Don't forget, Chiang: a nobleman is not one who has conquered the great passions and extinguished them — that is a saint or a wise man. Nor is he one conquered by passions — that is but a brute. A nobleman is one who has many passions and can subdue them, and he who can subdue them for a great Purpose is a king.

The time has come for me to subdue my passions for the great Purpose. The time has come for me to take authority.

(To his escort.)

The conch!

(His escort blows on the conch. At once the whole vision dissolves, the Magician removes his yellow mask, the first set re-appears; the crowd, as though awakening from a deep sleep, shake themselves and rub their eyes.)

PEOPLE   O Buddha, don't leave!

Buddha, take us with you, don't go!
He's gone!

MANDARIN   *(Jumps up, frightened.)*
It's Chiang!

PEOPLE   *(With fear.)*
It's Chiang! Chiang!
(Chiang approaches his old father.)

MANDARIN   Now the two beasts — father and son — will come to blows. I'll get closer to speak to him...I'm old, I know much, it's my duty!

CHIANG   *(To his escort who is blowing the conch.)*
Stop!

MANDARIN   *(Falling at Chiang's feet.)*
Don't raise the whip, Chiang; these are your people! Don't bite your lips in anger; it is your old father!
He once tore out a fistful of his body and molded you; he took up the end of the chain, joined you to the Ancestors — and made you immortal.
Bow and worship him, Chiang!

CHIANG   *(Pushing back the Mandarin with disdain.)*
Go!

MANDARIN   Respect the great Laws, Chiang, that keep the world from falling into chaos!

CHIANG   I respect the great Laws and trample on the small; I am thirty-five years old, on the peak of my ascent! My turn has come.

OLD MAN   *(Still dazed from the vision.)*
Who is it? Throw him out! Who blew on the holy vision and extinguished it?

CHIANG   I did!

LI-LIANG   Master, I bow and worship your power. Welcome.

CHIANG   Mother of my son, stand up. Don't bow down before me; you're not a slave, you're my wife. You bore a son, and may raise your head before kings.

LI-LIANG	Your slave in life and death, my Lord; I want no other glory.
OLD MAN	Who is it? I hear a voice, I see no one; I see Buddha in the air still, like golden flower-dust...
	Who are you, great denier? Who let out a shrill cry and shouted: "No!"?
CHIANG	*(Taking a step forward.)*
	It's your son, father!
OLD MAN	I hear, I tell you, but I can't see; the eyes of my flesh have been blinded, praise God! The eyes of my soul have opened, praise God!
	The entire air is a silken saffron flag on which Buddha is embroidered.
	Who are you?
	(He rises, looks, then steps back in horror.)
	You! You! Ah, the flag is torn, the stones have appeared again, and the soil, and the filthy deeds of man!
	O Ancestors,
	(He looks at the empty stools at right and left.)
	O Ancestors, alas, this is my son!
LI-LIANG	*(Opening her arms pleadingly to Chiang.)*
	Master, husband, I beg of you, don't be angry; he's the last god of your race, untouched, sacred, full of secret powers —
	He's your father.
	One of his feet is still on earth, the other is already climbing up the iconostasis where the Ancestors lie enthroned...Bow down and worship him!
CHIANG	I know my duty to my parents; I know my duty to my parents; I know how far reverence must go; don't be afraid,
	Li-Liang, I beg of you, go suckle your son; that is your duty; we must exchange manly words here.
MANDARIN	Oh, he's reaching out his hand for his father; the world is crumbling!
OLD MAN	*(Stepping back angrily.)*
	Why are you reaching out for me? What do you want of me?
CHIANG	The thing you hold — the staff of authority.

MUSICIANS   Ooh!
            (For a while, wild, muffled music.)

OLD MAN   *(Raising his staff high.)*
            I've not died yet.

CHIANG   You have died, father, you have died. Your eyes are still
                open, your mouth still emits a sound, you tread stones and
                the stones still move,
            But your soul has died, old Chiang, it has died!

OLD MAN   I have not died! I have not died! I live and I rule!

CHIANG   You're dead, father, you're dead, your day's work is done, it's
                my turn now! Both your feet are already in the grave. I'm
                still whole on the earth, my turn has come. Every
                generation has its own duty — the one to leave, the other to
                rule, the third to wait.
            It's my turn to rule.

OLD MAN   Put down your hands! I will not surrender; I call on the
                Ancestors: Help!

CHIANG   I call on the Descendants: Drive him away!

OLD MAN   I will not leave!

CHIANG   I can't talk with old men; their veins are blocked and won't let
                the blood pass through; the ditches of their brains are
                blocked and won't let the soul pass through; life has turned
                to gangrene in their thighs and their brains.
            Forgive me, old Chiang, I want power and power wants me;
                don't stand in my way!
            *(Old Koag advances, bows, goes to give the sword to the Old
            Man. With a blow, Chiang throws him down, but
            immediately regrets it.)*
            I didn't mean to do that, old Koag, forgive me...
            (To his escort.)
            Take him away.

OLD MAN   Ancestors, help me!

CHIANG   *(Grabs the sword, breaks it, and holds out the sheath to the
            Old Man.)*
            Your soul has died, old Chiang, and the sheath is empty;

62

take it.

Go into the Tower, wash and comb your hair, perfume it, then call on the Ancestors. Open your ledgers and give an accounting; tomorrow at dawn, with the new sun, I shall seize power.

OLD MAN   *(Beating his staff on the ground.)*
Ancestors, help!

CHIANG   *(Laughing sarcastically.)*
Shout, shout, they can't hear! Just now at Buddha's Monastery I threw them out of their graves, I heaped their bones, set them on fire, and scattered their ashes over the earth — there is no better fertilizer for good crops.
In the same way — so be it! — may our worthy sons scatter us, when the hour comes.

MANDARIN   We're lost! Life no longer has a foundation. How can it survive? The world is falling apart!
(The Old Man raises his staff, froths at the mouth, and his words become confused.)

LI-LIANG   *(Falling at the feet of the Old Man.)*
Father, set aside your rage; you are a nobleman.

OLD MAN   Traitor! You've sold your soul to the White Demons; you've broken the holy chain of the Ancestors!
You dress, you eat, you laugh, you talk, you fight like the Westerners, rebel!
(Turns to Young Koag.)
The whip!
(To Buddha)
He's reached the summit of evil. Buddha, give him a push, crush him.
(To Young Koag.)
The whip!

MANDARIN   Master, give me permission to speak.
(Shows his book.)
It's written here: "When the people raise their heads, the world is lost." Harmony! Harmony!

MAGICIAN   Don't come between them, penpusher! Let the beasts fight; that's why God gave them claws, teeth, horns — to fight

63

with.

Chiang, you're off, leaping toward the precipice — and there's nothing I can do for you. What help can one give a great soul? None! None!

It asks for the impossible, as it should. It leaps to its destruction, as it should — that is the meaning of a great soul, Chiang.

You've reached the edge of the precipice: Jump!

CHIANG   I overthrow old Chiang and seize power!

I abolish the worship of Ancestors and erect the worship of Descendants. We shall no longer look back, we shall look forward.

I sense one country within me, better than this country outside me, and I don't want to die before my eyes see people, plains, and rivers as I want them.

(He turns to the people.)

Brothers, brothers, come with me! Follow me, I bring you salvation.

PEOPLE   We don't want to be saved, we don't! Saved from what? From slavery, from injustice, from hunger? We're used to them now, we've adjusted, let us alone!

Let us alone! We were born to plow the earth, that noblemen might eat; to plow woman, that the Master's slaves might multiply.

Freedom? Salvation? Heroism? These are anxieties for noblemen. We're not noblemen, let us alone!

Let us alone! We bow and worship the great powers — the rain, the wind, the river, the caterpillar that eats our cabbage, the worm that eats our apples, the Master who eats them all. We want no more cares; let us alone!

Let us alone! Why do you want to disturb the order? Everything is fine; hunger, poverty, injustice, filth, and even the Master's whip, the shivering cold of winter and the heat of summer —

Everything's fine, everything, everything! Don't disturb the order; let us alone!

CHIANG   I will not let you alone!

(Slowly.)

My heart, do not forget, we've reached an agreement: you

64

	must not break!
MANDARIN	Eh, Chiang, listen to me, to this old man also. You'll be destroyed, Chiang, because you're concerned about saving others; such audacity belongs only to the gods... What are we? Men, little people, each man out for himself!
OLD MAN	*(Pacing back and forth in a fury, shouting.)* The whip! The whip! *(Young Koag appears from the tower with a whip.)* Bring it here!
LI-LIANG	*(Embracing the Old Man.)* Don't father! Think of Buddha! Here before us still, his holy cart shakes in the wind...Can't you see the black swan, father?
OLD MAN	I see nothing; don't hold me back. Buddha was an evening cloud filled with air. It has scattered! This one is flesh and bones; I will strike him!
LI-LIANG	You're a nobleman...
OLD MAN	I'm a nobleman; it's my duty to strike.
MAGICIAN	Strike!
OLD MAN	*(Raises his whip in fury.)* My curse upon you! *(Overcome with rage, he rushes toward Chiang, like a bull. Chiang draws back; the Old Man loses his balance, rolls on the ground, tears his clothing as foam rims his mouth. Frightened, the people surround him.)*
PEOPLE	The evil has hit him again! The great sickness of his clan has struck him. He's foaming at the mouth; his eyes have turned white!
CHIANG	Cover him!
LI-LIANG	*(Covers the Old Man with her shawl; turns to the crowd.)* For shame, don't look! *(To the Magician.)* Beloved and skillful exorcist, I beg of you: Drive off the evil spirits, that his soul may return to its familiar body.
MAGICIAN	My Noble Lady, bring him your son, I have no other spell;

	bring him his only grandchild – he will look at it and his soul will return to entwine itself once more with its beloved flesh.
LI-LIANG	I shall go. *(Leaves hurriedly toward the Tower.)*
MAGICIAN	The crowd is right in fearing for its salvation; the old man is right in resisting; you, too, are right to be in a hurry, Chiang; that is your duty.

The better you carry out your duty, the nearer you approach your destruction; that's the way it is. If you were not so great a soul, if you were a bit cowardly, if you forgot, or if you failed a little – what happiness!

But you do not condescend, great soul! I like you!

CHIANG: Sly monk, you too, are like your master, Buddha. You look at the world and burst into laughter.

PEOPLE: Silence...silence...Li-Liang is bringing her son.

CHIANG: Don't hurry, Li-Liang, my soul wants to leave, too – but this child holds it back. Wait a moment, I want to see his face...
(Looks at his son and his face lights up for a moment.)
Thank you, Li-Liang, go now...
(Pushes her toward the Old Man. To himself:)
This is my son; this is the world to come, the real, certain god of earth – I bow and worship his grace!

LI-LIANG: *(Kneeling.)*
Father...father...open your eyes, it's your grandson!

OLD MAN: *(Opens his eyes, lets out a happy cry.)*
Ah!

LI-LIANG: Take him in your arms, father...

OLD MAN: No, my breath can still poison; take him!
(Sits up and covers his face with his hands.)
O, Ancestors, forgive me; for a moment I lost the balance of nobility.
Hu-Ming, Buddha's words have gone for nothing...His cart has vanished, the great disciples have vanished, the black swan has flown away...To my shame, I could not rein in

my fury.
(To his son.)
Eh, Chiang, Chiang, help me put my heart in order, say a
good word to bring me peace.
Why do you look at me in silence? You betrayed the
Ancestors! You are no longer Chinese, you've not yet
become a Westerner; you're in the middle, like a mule!
Your panoply will not be hung,
No, it will not be hung beside the panoplies of the Ancestors.
I cursed you with every bone in my body, Chiang!

CHIANG   I accept it, old Chiang; may my son, one day, too, leave me
so far behind and frighten me so that I, too, may give him
my curse.
There is no better blessing for the young; thank you, father.

OLD MAN   Out of my sight! I cast you from our race; I cast you from
our graves, from my home's hearth, from my courtyard's
well, from the ancient threshold of our ancestors. Go!

CHIANG   I'm not a dog to be shouted at and slink away; I'm not a bird
to fly dangling in the air;
I'm a tree, and my roots plunge deep into the yellow mud of
China. I will not go!

OLD MAN   You made a son; I have my grandson; I don't need you.
(He holds his grandchild up to the full moon.)
O round moon, sweet sun of night, thrice-noble youth of the
sky,
Spread out your lily hands, caress my grandchild, fill his
palms with silver; his entrails are overflowing with milk.
This is my grandson!
I place the whole world on one side of the scale, the five seas,
the seven shores, the nine strata of the wind, and on the
other, this small piece of flesh.
I have no other hope in the world.
*(Wild, frightened music; the First Sentry enters, muddy from
head to toe.)*

PEOPLE   The First Sentry of the river! He must be bringing terrible
news. Look, he's all muddy!
His lips tremble, he cannot speak!
He speaks; be quiet!

67

FIRST SENTRY   Master, brothers...O my general, Chiang!

OLD MAN   Don't speak to him! My curse spilled over his body like
            leprosy; don't speak to him!
            (Raises the staff of authority.)
            I am the master and the father of my people. I will account to
            the Ancestors when I descend into the ground; I am the
            lips, the ears, the brain of the land. Speak to *me!*
            Raise your eyes Sentry, look at me; I grant you permission.

FIRST SENTRY   Master...Master...

OLD MAN   What are those agitated waters that rise and fall in your eyes?

FIRST SENTRY   It's the river Yangtze, the dreadful Blue River, Master.

OLD MAN   It's the mighty god of the land; I bow and worship to its
            grace. Speak!

FIRST SENTRY   I'm choking, I can't speak, I'm afraid.
            Swear that you'll not raise your whip, Master.

OLD MAN   Speak!

FIRST SENTRY   You will not swear?

OLD MAN   I will not swear; speak!

FIRST SENTRY   Three days and three nights, Master, I didn't close my eyes.
            Bent over my lookout, I gazed down
            Where the Westerners further on were completing the third,
            the final dam to hold back our river, our mighty god, the
            Yangtze. Their cursed machines glistened, groaned and
            filled the air with smoke.
            The Yangtze was silent; it flowed, peacefully, thickly, deeply,
            and it didn't speak. It's a god, you see, and it was patient.
            It restrained its strength and did not condescend to pay the
            slightest attention to men.
            But I, who understand its nature, looked at it and trembled...
            Don't drown us, my God, I murmured as I trembled, don't
            drown us, my God...

OLD MAN   You talk too much; lean against the wall or you'll fall; be
            brief.

FIRST SENTRY   Let me speak, Master, let me unburden myself...I'm afraid and
            I can't gather my wits together to know what I should say

and what I should not...

And suddenly there were songs and joyous rifle shots until the tents of the Westerners shook. I turned and looked. They had finished their task; they had harnessed the river with enormous breakwaters; they were laughing, dancing and making merry.

I leaned over and what did I see? The god shuddered, his back reddened, laughter broke out far and wide, and for thousands of yards, to the left and the right, the earth began to crack...I didn't think of anything dreadful...It must be playing, I said...

But the next day, at dawn, my lookout began to shake...I leaned down but saw darkness only. I could see nothing, but I heard a terrible roar; the waters were not laughing any longer; they were groaning, threatening, beating against the barriers, knocking down plane-trees, rising higher and higher...

And on the third day...the third day...

OLD MAN Speak! Go on! I'm glad! Good health to you, Almighty Dragon with your blue fish-scales!

The Westerners thought they could harness you, and this one here brought them, with their impious, grimy machines that contaminate the pure air of China.

O Almighty Dragon with your blue fish-scales, your green eyes, your yellow teeth, Great Ancestor!

(To Chiang.)

Why are you laughing?

CHIANG We chained your dragon, the Yangtze, with stones, cement and iron — three chains. It, too, will enter the service of man.

OLD MAN *(Frightened at the blaspheming, he covers his ears.)*
I heard nothing! O Yangtze, you hear everything — and I surrender him to you!

PEOPLE O Yangtze, long-bearded grandfather, you bring us life — rice, corn, watermelon, cotton, sugar cane; you bring us fishes, eels, barges and boats...

You bring us the great shadows — the sun, the moon, the birds, the clouds — and take them out to sea...

Enough! Enough! Don't bring us death, too!

OLD MAN   Don't start the dirges! God detests the man who weeps.
          (To the Sentry.)
          Speak! Your mouth is still full.

FIRST SENTRY   The third day, Master...on the third day the waters turned
               green, red, black; they knocked down the plane trees, they
               foamed and laughed, until my lookout became a boat
               floating on the waters...
               Master, don't raise your whip; it's not my fault.

OLD MAN   Speak! Speak!

FIRST SENTRY   On the third day the Westerners laid out huge tables on the
               high terraces of the temple, slaughtered the sacred geese
               from the Yangtze Monastery, removed the taps from its
               wine-barrels — and began to eat and drink.
               The Westerners ate and drank, vomited and ate again; they
               threw the bones, the peelings, the wine dregs into the river
               and laughed raucously. "Here, here," they shouted to the
               river: "eat!"
               And the Old God accepted all and swallowed all; but
               suddenly, as the Westerners rose from their tables,
               unbuttoned, bare-headed and befuddled with drink,
               The cataracts of the sky opened, Master, the cataclysm burst,
               Master, the waters swelled, rose and fell, and the peasants
               rushed between the river and the first barrier, loaded
               themselves with food, tools, clothing, babies — and ran off!
               They picked up their tubs, their cradles, their gods — and
               they ran off!
               It's raining, it's raining on your villages, Master, and the
               people and the houses are dissolving, they're turning back
               into mud again...

OLD MAN   O Yangtze, do not drown my people. Stop to distinguish
          between them. The Westerners are the White Demons —
          drown *them!* These yellow bodies here are my people,
          Yangtze, they are your children, Yangtze, mud of your
          mud, have mercy!

FIRST SENTRY   Mothers gathered their babies to their breasts, girls opened
               their hope-chests and said goodbye to their dowries,

And your daughter, Master, your daughter Mei-Ling...

OLD MAN   My daughter Mei-Ling?
           (To Chiang.)
           May you be cursed! You went to widen a woman's heart, but
               you broke it!

CHIANG   *(Grasps the Sentry's shoulder.)*
           Speak! My sister Mei-Ling? Come closer!

OLD MAN   Speak to *me!* My daughter Mei-Ling?

FIRST SENTRY   She won't eat, she won't drink, she won't sleep, Master...She
                runs from village to village ringing the bells, shouting...

OLD MAN   What is she shouting? Why did you stop?
           (Laughs bitterly.)
           You think I can't bear it? Speak, I can bear it! What is she
               shouting?

FIRST SENTRY   Just what her brother Chiang is shouting, Master..."Stones,
                cement and iron," she shouts, "don't be afraid! Stones,
                cement and iron" — and she mocks the almighty god, the
                Yangtze...

MUSICIANS *(They play in fear, then as they see the peasants arriving, they*
           shout:)
           Oh! Oh! Oh!
           (The peasants arrive soaked, drenched with mud, carrying
           bundles and babies. They wail as they look, terrified, behind
           them.)

PEASANTS   It's coming! It's coming! It's coming!

PEOPLE   Who! Who!

PEASANTS   The Yangtze. It broke the first barrier and sank our villages...
               A curse on whoever's to blame!
           A curse on whoever's to blame! I dug, I planted, I watered; I
               waited. I waited for the sun, the rain, the weather — the
               three great noblemen. I waited, I trusted. I knew
           That this is the grindstone: plowing, planting, waiting...I said:
               the harvest will come.
           But the river came and swept everything away! A curse on
               whoever's to blame!

71

OLD MAN	Who's to blame? Raise your eyes, look at me!
PEASANTS	A curse on whoever's to blame!
MAGICIAN	Peasants, people, courage! You will see even more terrible things; this is only the beginning; but later
	You'll see killings, drownings, love-making, you will see gods weeping — courage, my children!
	You'll see the Yangtze itself opening this very door and entering. Steel your hearts to bear it; say secretly to yourselves: "It's only a game, my heart, only a game, don't be afraid."
	Do you hear? That's what you must say, that's the secret of enduring life; to face death, sickness, injustice, fear, and to say: "It's a game, my heart, a game, don't be afraid."
MANDARIN	Accursed tongue, stop speaking! Chiang has grown pale, he's pushing through the crowd, seeking his sister Mei-Ling.
CHIANG	(Runs, opens his arms)
	Mei-Ling!
	(The sky becomes cloudy; the moon is hidden; thunder is heard from afar; blue lightning tears through the air; the storm approaches. Mei-Ling, drenched, gasping, falls into the arms of her brother. Chiang caresses her tenderly.)
	Sister, comrade who stood beside me, Mei-Ling.
	(Music, all passion and gentleness.)
MAGICIAN	(Looking insatiably at Mei-Ling, to the Mandarin.)
	What are the white candles doing here? Why is she dressed like a bride?
MANDARIN	You can't mingle with the spirits and go unpunished...You're dreaming, or you're seeing things — what candles?
MAGICIAN	What are the white candles doing here? Don't you see them? Why is she dressed like a bride?
	(Brother and sister gaze at and caress each other with inexpressible love.)
MEI-LING	Chiang, Chiang, my brother!
CHIANG	Hold your head high, Mei-Ling...
MEI-LING	Chiang, my brother, the first barrier has broken...
	(Silence.)
	They're gone, my brother, the villages that followed our

lead are drowned...They no longer drank or smoked hashish, or gambled...

For years they struggled, brother, for years, and now...in one night...

CHIANG The people around us are watching; raise your head high, my sister.

OLD MAN Mei-Ling!

MEI-LING The Old Man is calling me — I don't want to speak to him, I don't!

CHIANG Go to him, Mei-Ling, he's old, don't mind him; he's old, and behind the times;
Speak softly to him as we speak to the dead.

OLD MAN Mei-Ling!
(Mei-Ling approaches with restrained anger.)
I'm listening.

MEI-LING I've nothing to say.

OLD MAN *(Ironically.)*
You've nothing to say?

MEI-LING I have. The Yangtze has broken the first dam, it's drowned the villages, it's risen to a man's height above the rooftops — you've got what you wanted.

OLD MAN *(Turns to his daughter-in-law.)*
I'm falling apart inside, Li-Liang.

LI-LIANG *(Holds him in her arms so he will not fall.)*
Father...

OLD MAN Ah!...The God of China has stirred and crushed the Westerners!
(To Mei-Ling.)
Yes, that's what I wanted, that! I cried out, and my God heard me!

PEOPLE Master, save us! You are our Nobleman; it's your duty. You always had three bowls, three cups, three beds, but also three swords — a triple portion of joy, but also a triple portion of danger.
Nobleman, find out who's to blame and strike him; strike him

73

	and save your people.
OLD MAN	Don't shout — put your hands down!
PEASANTS	Strike him, whoever he is, and save your people; that is the meaning of Master!
	Listen, God thunders, he speaks; listen to him!
OLD MAN	My entrails are filled with drowning villages, and I am myself a sinking province.
	(Turns to a mother who opens her mouth to speak.)
	Silence, shut your mouth, that shameless wound! You speak your pain and are relieved, but I must take it all within me.
	You shed tears and empty your hearts, but I am a nobleman, and I can't weep...I mustn't! The tears accumulate inside me, they can't open a channel to escape — I'm drowning!
	(Paces back and forth groaning; muffled music is heard. Suddenly he leaps toward his son.)
	You're to blame! You! You! You! You brought these new shameful gods here, and our old gods have grown angry; they've armed themselves and are descending!
	(Raises his whip, strikes Chiang on the face furiously.)
	May you be cursed!
MAGICIAN	*(Joyfully.)*
	Ah! The wheel spins. Fate rolls up her sleeves to rush into the fray!
PEOPLE	*(With dread.)*
	He struck his son!
	He struck his son in the face with a whip!
	Blood spurted!
	Back! Back! Now the two beasts will come to grips!
	Make way for them!
	(Chiang starts, steps back, wipes the blood as it spreads over his face, then grasps the knife in his belt, holding the handle tightly, biting his lips. Abruptly he pushes back the Mandarin who has risen and is trying to block him and Li-Liang. He continues, slowly, craftily, toward the Old Man.)
MEI-LING	*(Crouched.)*
	Strike!
PEOPLE	Listen, the thunder approaches, the earth trembles...He's going

74

to kill the Old Man now!
Look how the knife throbs in Chiang's fist!

MEI-LING   Strike!
               (*Li-Liang touches Chiang's arm, pleadingly, but he twists
               away, pushing her back. Mei-Ling rushes to Li-Liang and
               pushes her aside. For a moment the two women glare at each
               other with hatred. Chiang fixes his eyes on the Old Man who
               stands erect and waits. Wild music. Old Koag runs and brings
               the Old Man a new sword, but with a violent movement the
               Old Man pushes him back.*)

MEI-LING   Strike!
               (*Chiang has finally reached the Old Man but passes him by,
               barely touching him provokingly, then proceeds and reaches
               the closed door of the Tower. He stops, lets out a shrill cry
               like a vulture and then with sudden fury plunges the dagger
               into the Tower door and leaves it there, erect. The First
               Musician rises, bows to the audience, takes down the gong
               and strikes it hard, once. Curtain.*)

               (End of Act I)

ACT II

(*Dawn. The large hall of the Tower. On the wall hang the Ancestors' seven panoplies, with death masks covering the faces, and black-handled daggers thrust in the belts. Beneath them is a narrow balcony along the length of the wall. From the center and back the area is raised in three steps; an open curtain divides the area in two. Far back is a huge statue of Buddha with three-fold bellies and overlapping chins, bursting with laughter. There are three doors: one behind Buddha, a large one to the left, and a low one to the right. Dim lights. The canary in the cage has awakened and is warbling. The three musicians are sitting cross-legged in their places, to the right, playing and creating the mood. The Old Man is sitting cross-legged on the balcony under the panoplies, smoking a long pipe. A seven-branched oil lamp glows weakly before him. To his right and left, relieved of their panoplies, the seven Ancestors sit. The Old Man watches them anxiously.*)

OLD MAN   Has no one found him innocent? No one? O Terrible
    Ancestors, don't you pity him?
(*Points to the low door at right.*)
There, inside there, he sleeps in his ancestral home with the
    trust of a child...Listen to his breathing. It's soft and
    peaceful, like a baby's.
For months now he's been roaming the villages and fighting,
    he too, in his own way, to help the people.
He may be wrong, lawless, I know, but his heart is pure, O
    Ancestors, pure and clean, I swear!
Open his heart, open and look, what do you see?
Our China,
Our country with her fields and villages, with rivers, with
    gravestones...Happiness...Happiness...Our country is in his
    heart, as green as an emerald,
Wealthy villages, clean streets, harbors filled with ships,
    thresholds filled with children — and peaceful smoke rising
    from every hut.
Within his heart, O Ancestors, is the perfect China, the future
    China, strong and happy,
Drinking his blood and casting up its first sprouts.
Have mercy, Ancestors, pity him; he's tired and he's come at

night to lean against you, O immortal dead, to gather strength, to go further on.

Lean over his bed, look at his face, lean a little more, look into his heart.

You gaze upon him and say: "He's wild, cruel, he loves bloodshed; but inside, his heart is tender, fresh, like the heart of the sugar cane."

Here,

(Takes out a paper from inside his shirt.)

Here are a few of his rhymes, for he, too,

(Turns left.)

Like you, father, loves to weave songs, to ease his heart when it overflows.

Listen to what I found on his table the other day...

(He reads.)

> *Fields, mountains, and serenity!*
> *It's raining, and the land*
> *Drinks sweetly and quiescently.*
> *Ah, I saw you stand*
> *Misted in your sunny rain,*
> *Your face wet in a strange blend,*
> *Weeping and laughing once again,*
> *O fatherland!*

(He watches the Ancestors anxiously. They remain unmoving, silent. The soft sound of a knife being sharpened is heard.)

Eh, my tongue is sore from pleading and shouting all night; I'm weary of it! It's not proper for me to speak and not be answered.

I'm like you, too, Chiang; I, too, have my weapons, and above the doorway of my tower, and on my silken banner and gold seal is the same ancestral monogram as yours:

(Makes a forceful gesture in the air.)

A tiger!

Eh, Ancestors, I stamp my foot; give me a sure sign! Not your slanted, customary chewed-up words, but speak clearly so I will know what to do!

The spirits fly in a straight line; they speak to me honorably and frankly, like men.

(Silence. The sound of a knife being sharpened grows louder.)

Oh, don't make me do something terrible, something I'll regret later!

Eh, old men, be careful! I seem good, soft, I restrain my
hands, I don't kill — but don't awaken the beast in me...
(Beats his chest.)
In here sleeps a yellow tiger with black stripes — be careful!
(Turns to the right.)
Grandfather, you spent all your life fighting to free the
people...They were beasts, you wanted to make them men;
they were slaves, you wanted to make them free.
And the day your first son was born, my father, you gathered
seven thousand slaves from your fields, seven thousand
souls, and as one opens up a cage, you stretched out your
hand and freed them. Open your mouth now, grandfather,
and say a kind word.
(Points to the low door.)
And this great-grandson of yours follows in your footsteps;
he, too, struggles like you to do good to the numberless
swarm of China. He, too, fights like you — your great
breath churns within him. He wants to turn it into fruit
that you may be glad your seed was not scattered to the
winds.
Let him go, and we'll see; give him time, grandfather, he's
young, his blood is still boiling. Give him time to settle, to
find the right path — your path, O Ancestors!
(The sharpening of the knife now is heard more loudly.)
Eh, eh, stop sharpening the knife! Enough! Let him live, I say!
A great heart but unsubdued; a great virtue but without
discipline. He's young. That is the meaning of being young.
Give him time, grandfather, to mature, to recover from the
divine sickness — youth!
All of us, if you remember, were young once. We, too,
wanted to tear down the world and rebuild it; our blood
was like wine-must, it boiled. The time came, the boiling
stopped, the must cleared, it became wine. Keep your trust
in youth.
Ancestors, god-protectors of our lineage, I bow and worship
you. I've told you what I wanted; my heart has emptied,
my brain has emptied — judge now, decide!
Grandfather, speak first!
(The Grandfather stretches out his hand, grasps the knife that
was being sharpened and wedges it into the hand of the Old
Man. The Old Man is startled, and the knife drops to the
ground. The canary, disquieted, begins to sing.)

Oh!

(Turns to the Ancestor to his left and touches his knee.)

Father! You were good, sweet, you loved all living things, the birds, the flowers, the people. You took the quill and wrote songs on silk. And your closed heart opened as a garden opens, with blossoming tangerine trees, and you strolled through it.

And at other times you held in your arms this son of mine, Chiang, and danced him in your lap and said what I say now to my grandson: "I have no other hope in the world."

And here he is now; your grandson has grown big and strong, he's become a man — listen, lean over so I can tell you, that your heart may rejoice: he has the same voice as you, the same height, the same walk...

The old men look at him, open their eyes wide and say: "His grandfather has been resurrected! His grandfather has risen from the earth!" And now,

You've heard what I've prayed for all night, father...I spoke of him, your grandson: pity him. Open your mouth, say a kind word!

(The father puts out his hand slowly, silently, grabs the knife from the floor, thrusts it in the fist of the Old Man. The Old Man lets out a cry, throws the knife away and rises, staggering.)

You, too? You, too? I have one thing more to say to you, O terrible Ancestors! One word, one last word...

(But at that moment the roosters begin to crow, and the Ancestors dissolve in air. The Old Man looks around him, bewildered, throws his pipe away, and rubs his eyes.)

Ooh! With whom was I talking? Who was I begging? Who placed this knife in my hand? Why do my lips drip poison? O dark powers, O voices of my heart!

(Looks at the panoplies.)

Listen to me, Ancestors, don't cloud my brain! Don't howl like jackals in the night! Speak clearly, like men. I'm not a slave to be afraid; I'm not a woman to be compassionate; I'm not one who wants to escape without paying his debt.

I'm a demon too, like all of you; I'm a Chiang, too,

I uproot my heart from my chest —

And I pay!

(The roar of the river is heard.)

Who roars?

(Jumps away from the window. The roar of the river is heard clearly, distant tolling bells, thunder. The Old Man listens.)

Hold on, old Chiang! Hold on, old Chiang! Don't be afraid. The river roars below, God roars above, and you stand between them. Roar, too!

Who placed this sharpened knife in my fist? Who took it from the Ancestors' panoplies?

(Raises the lantern and looks at the panoplies.)

Oh, it's gone from the savage grandfather's iron belt!

(Steps back, murmuring with horror.)

No! No! No!

(Approaches the low door, listens.)

He's sleeping...I hear his breathing like that of a small child's...It's peaceful, peaceful.

Beloved rebel, if you only knew! This whole night I've been fighting all the terrible shadows for you...

(Throws the knife on the balcony, opens his eyes wide, looks at it with terror, shouts.)

I won't! I won't!

(Abruptly the musicians begin to play. To the left, the large door opens, the First Sentry enters, mud-splattered. The Old Man recovers and raises his head calmly.)

I'm listening.

FIRST SENTRY   Master...

OLD MAN   Don't be afraid, speak. Look I've just risen from the earth; my mouth and throat and my entrails are filled with death, and I endure. Speak, then; don't be afraid!

Did you go to the villages I sent you? Did you see?

FIRST SENTRY   I saw.

OLD MAN   Well? I'm listening.

FIRST SENTRY   Master, the world is turning to mud again...God regretted creating man, God regretted creating the animals and the trees, and it rains, it rains, it rains...

O God, you're turning the world back into mud again!

OLD MAN   Leave God alone. If you have something to say, say it to me, and I'll tell God.

This is what order means! What did you see with your eyes,

slave, that's what I ask you. Anything beyond that is not your concern.

FIRST SENTRY Master, the river is angry, it swells and tears down the shore; the valley has become a lake, and drums, sheep, dogs and cows are floating in it.

OLD MAN Not so loud, don't shout; there are women here, they might hear. Go on! Forget the sheep, the dogs, the cows; it's the people I pity, the souls.
What happened to the people? Speak!

FIRST SENTRY They're floating in the water, Master, on their backs, with their feet toward the sea...From yellow they've turned green, from green to black; crows swoop upon them and eat their eyes.

OLD MAN Nothing else? Nothing else? There's still more poison on your lips; you've turned green.

FIRST SENTRY I'm afraid...

OLD MAN (*Frightened, grabs his arm.*)
Did you see anything? A large phantom? Did he give you any orders for me?
That's it, that's it! I see it in your eyes! What orders?
(*To himself.*)
Hold fast, my heart!

FIRST SENTRY Master, just now, at dawn, I saw...

OLD MAN Don't stammer. Close the door, close the window so I can hear.

FIRST SENTRY I saw phantoms on the water, moaning...They were full of foam and seaweed...they rose and fell, with big mustaches stiff with anger.
They roared, they threatened, they rushed toward your Tower, Master, I swear...And they wore...

OLD MAN Why do you look at the wall with fear? Speak! They wore...

FIRST SENTRY ...These panoplies, Master...these exactly! And they roared and shouted, and I heard your name! Your name and the name of your son!

OLD MAN Oh! Oh! Didn't they ask you to tell me something? To give

81

me some order? Didn't they say: "Tell the Old Man..."

FIRST SENTRY   No, no! They didn't even turn to look at me. They passed in
                front of me, staggering and stumbling over one another.
                They thundered, they mounted the river and descended.

OLD MAN   Remember well.
                (Grabs his shoulder.)
                Tell the truth! They said nothing, nothing?

FIRST SENTRY   I swear, Master, nothing...

OLD MAN   *(Sighs in deep relief.)*
                Thank God!

FIRST SENTRY   They merely sighed, Master, and rumbled like buffaloes.

OLD MAN   And then? Then? Try to remember.

FIRST SENTRY   I don't know — the cocks crowed, they disappeared...

OLD MAN   Go!

FIRST SENTRY   Master, I have one more thing to say — give me permission to
                speak freely...

OLD MAN   Freely? Where did you learn that word? How did it pass the
                frontiers of China and enter here?
                I will raise breakwaters, I will build towers, I will open
                trenches to keep foreign demons from entering my fields.
                Lower your eyes — no one looks at a nobleman above the
                chest...Even lower. Speak now, what do you want? You
                have my permission.

FIRST SENTRY   Master, I'd like to speak of my pain...You said: "I've returned
                from the earth and carry death in my entrails." — I, too,
                have returned from the waters, Master, and I carry death
                in my entrails. If you would condescend to look into my
                eyes,
                You will see them filled with drowned people.

OLD MAN   Very well, very well, I see them! I've heard the message you
                bring me; it's entered my blood — leave us alone now, them
                and me, to fight!
                Why do you hesitate? Do you carry more poison?

FIRST SENTRY   Nobleman, the people cling to you. This is what everyone is

82

	shouting, wherever I go. They look to you, Master, they expect much from you.
OLD MAN	Expect what?
FIRST SENTRY	Salvation...They say you are savage, but good and just. Dressed in silk, you eat and drink in peace under the green trees in summer, beside the hearth in winter, as your people work safely under your shadow. Where there is danger, you are the first to enter.
OLD MAN	I know; raise your eyes, look! *(Opens his chest.)* My body is filled with wounds, from head to toe. I've done my duty.
FIRST SENTRY	*(Slowly, trembling.)* It's not enough...
OLD MAN	*(Restraining his fury with difficulty.)* What?
FIRST SENTRY	*(Trembling.)* It's not enough.
OLD MAN	Not enough?
FIRST SENTRY	You're a great nobleman, Master, and you know the secret the smaller noblemen do not know...
OLD MAN	What secret?
FIRST SENTRY	That above manliness stands another, more brilliant virtue.
OLD MAN	You have something terrible on your mind, slave! Why do you choke on every word and swallow your tongue? What virtue?
FIRST SENTRY	*(Barely audible.)* Sacrifice.
OLD MAN	*(Worried, agonizingly.)* Sacrifice? What sacrifice?
FIRST SENTRY	Why do you ask? You know. You know very well who is to blame for infuriating the terrible god, the river.
OLD MAN	I don't know! Don't look at me; lower your eyes.

(Silence.)
Why do you shout?

FIRST SENTRY   I didn't shout, Master, I didn't speak.

OLD MAN   You shout from head to toe; go away so I won't hear you!

FIRST SENTRY   Master, it's not me you hear but the secret voice inside you...
And you know well, you know very well what I mean.

OLD MAN   *(Raising his hands in despair.)*
My God, don't give me all I can bear!
(To First Sentry.)
Go, I want to be alone with these.
(Points to the panoplies.)

FIRST SENTRY   I'm leaving, but my voice will remain, Master, because it's not
I who shout; it's you who are shouting, nobleman Chiang!
Better for one person to be lost, Master, than thousands!

OLD MAN   *(Leaps with sudden fury and shakes the Sentry by the
shoulders.)*
Go!
*(The Sentry leaves. The Old Man rushes toward the low
door, raises his hands.)*
My child!
*(Slowly steps back, drags himself toward the knife, wipes the
sweat from his brow, stares hypnotically at the knife on the
balcony, puts out his hand but draws it back again. Shouts.)*
Eh, eh, that's enough, you almighty dead, don't pull me — I'll
go no further!
*(The door at center depth opens. Quickly the Old Man leaps
for the knife, hides it inside his clothing against his chest and
holds it there tightly. Li-Liang steps out from behind the
statue of Buddha, carrying a tray with the morning's tea, and
stands on the first step, hesitating. The Old Man speaks,
softly.)*
Heart, old, ancient heart of Chiang, hold fast!

LI-LIANG   Father...

OLD MAN   Li-Liang...Go...Go...Pity me, Li-Liang-Go...
*(Li-Liang watches the Old Man as tears fall silently down her
cheeks. The Old Man shares her pain.)*
Come!

84

(Softer.)
Come, unfortunate girl, come...
(Li-Liang descends the three steps, kneels, places the tray down and bows. The Old Man kicks the tray over, spilling the tea. Li-Liang kneels at the Old Man's feet.)

LI-LIANG   Father...

OLD MAN   Li-Liang, my child, forgive me, I'm in pain.

LI-LIANG   I know, father, all night I heard you sighing. You haven't slept all night, father.

OLD MAN   No, I was not sighing — I was talking.

LI-LIANG   You were talking, father?

OLD MAN   Get up, my dear, get up...
(Sighs.)
Man is a small island surrounded by waves, waves, waves of the dead. Another great storm is brewing tonight; they'll drown me, Li-Liang, the dead will drown me; help me!
No, no, don't stretch out your hand, don't open your mouth. I don't want help! You too, are a charming little island, the waves beat at you also, and there is no bridge...Why do you put out your hand? There is no bridge...
Don't cry; go, leave me alone. I'm talking with the Ancestors.

LI-LIANG   Let me stay in this corner, father; give me your permission.
I'll sit in a little heap, I won't speak, I won't cry — let me;
I won't look, I won't listen, let me...

OLD MAN   No, no, I'm talking with the male Ancestors. Women are not permitted here, Li-Liang;
We make decisions...
(Sighs deeply.)
We've found salvation.

LI-LIANG   What salvation, father?

OLD MAN   Be quiet!
(Looks worriedly toward the low door.)
Did he waken? Speak softly, my child.

LI-LIANG   What salvation, father?

OLD MAN   *(Worried.)*

85

Did he waken?

LI-LIANG   Why are you frightened, father? He's sleeping. He won't
            waken, poor dear; he's tired, going from village to village,
            gathering an army. He's had many cares — didn't you see
            him? He's wasted away.
            What salvation, father?

OLD MAN   Listen how the river roars! It's angry, it has swollen, it will
            drown my people. Open the window, my child, so I can
            hear it and take courage.
            (Li-Liang opens the window. The dreadful roar of the river
            is heard, the Old Man breathes deeply.)
            Ah! Ah! Welcome! He's a dreadful god, he does not forgive;
            they say he favors no one; he eats people...What do you
            say, Li-Liang?

LI-LIANG   There's only one thing I'm thinking of, father: what salvation?

OLD MAN   Li-Liang...

LI-LIANG   Command me!

OLD MAN   Do me a big favor, my child...

LI-LIANG   Command me, father.

OLD MAN   Bring me my grandchild. This loneliness is unbearable, this
            hour is hard to endure — bring me my grandchild!

LI-LIANG   He's sleeping. He, too, didn't rest all night, as though he were
            having an evil dream. He was babbling, shrieking like a
            bird,
            Then at dawn sleep finally came. Shall I wake him, father?

OLD MAN   Wake him; I want to see him, to touch him, to take courage
            ...Go on...
            (Pushes her gently, persistently.)
            Don't you pity me? Go on...

LI-LIANG   (Stands in agony.)
            Father, why do you send me away?
            (Embraces him, feels the handle of the knife against his chest,
            and lets out a harrowing cry.)
            Ah!
            (Falls at his feet and embraces his knees. The Old Man throws

86

the knife on the balcony.)

OLD MAN *(Caressing her hair.)*
Don't cry, don't cry, unfortunate child — there's no other
    salvation...All night we held court here; the Ancestors
    came, they stepped down from their panoplies; they sat
    here, look, here, to my right and left...
I talked and talked, I spoke till my tongue swelled from
    talking, my voice cracked from pleading and shouting...All
    night long, and now, see, just before the cocks crowed...

LI-LIANG Just before the cocks crowed?

OLD MAN The decision was reached. Quiet now, don't cry, pity me...

LI-LIANG The decision was reached?
*(Drags herself on her knees to the low door, stretches full-
length over the threshold, as though to block anyone from
passing through.)*

OLD MAN *(Raising his arms toward the panoplies.)*
O Ancestors, there's still time, give me a sign. Seize my hand,
    forbid me!
There, I will count to seven. O Ancestors, I give you time to
    give me a sign...To call me! No — don't! Rise! Come out of
    your graves, I'm counting!
*(Counts slowly, hoarsely, his voice trembling more with each
word. The loud regular beat of a drum accompanies each
word. The Old Man looks at the seven Ancestors on the wall,
one by one.)*
One — Two — Three — O Ancestors, O dreadful powers,
    mercy! Raise a shrill cry, let the doors creak, let Buddha
    shake his head, let a cry be heard in my skull, a No! I ask
    for a sign!
Four — Five — Nothing! Nothing!
Six...
(Approaches the window.)
It's raining, raining, the sky has exhausted itself, may it be
    cursed! Eh, Ancestors, are you deaf, are you mute? Give
    me a sign!
Ancestors, I've reached the edge of the precipice, I send you
    my last cry: Seven!
(Stands in agony watching the Ancestors. Savage music. The

87

canary is singing sweetly, joyfully. The Old Man bends and slyly walks toward the knife gleaming on the balcony. He looks at it with terror but an irresistible power pushes him. He groans, resists, but still advances, and then suddenly, driven almost insane, seizes the knife. With a powerful leap, wailing, he strides over Li-Liang, opens the door, enters and bolts it from inside. A few moments of silence. Li-Liang raises her head and listens. From inside comes the deep, heavy sigh of the Old Man, and then, suddenly, a harrowing scream.)

LI-LIANG   *(Leaps up and claws at the door, shaking it.)*
Help! Help!

OLD MAN   *(Opens the low door violently, rushes out in a daze, his hands dripping with blood, then leaps on the balcony and rubs the blood on the ancestral panoplies, groaning.)*
There, there, there! I rub your beards, your mouths, your
    nostrils, your neck; eat, eat and be satisfied!
O Almighty Gods, O voices out of the earth, I did what you
    wanted. I did what you wanted, alas for me!
(Crumbles to the ground, sighing.)
I did what you wanted; now keep your word too: Turn back
    the river so it won't drown my people!

LI-LIANG   *(Crouching, crawls to the threshold, kisses it, then enters the room of the murdered man.)*
I'm coming...I'm coming...I'm coming.

OLD MAN   *(Raises his head, listens. Silence for some time. The roar of the river is heard growing more savage.)*
No, no, it can't be, no! It's not the river! Didn't we agree?
    I've given it the guilty man! It ate, it's satisfied, it will calm
    down. I owed and I paid.
The Ancestors placed the knife in my hand, I thrust it into
    my heart! I did what they wanted, let them now do what
    I want!
(Listens again, then suddenly leaps up angrily.)
No, I tell you, it's not the river! O royal vein, be silent, that
    I may hear.
(Leans from the window, listens to the dreadful roar.)
It's the river, it's the Yangtze! Be patient a little longer, my
    heart, do not break. The Ancestors commanded, and they

do not lie; keep your trust!
(Suddenly a sarcastic laugh is heard behind him. He turns and looks at the statue of Buddha.)
Who laughed? You! You! O horrible, insatiable mouth of
    Nothingness, Buddha!
(Suddenly, as though a terrifying thought cuts through his mind, he claps his hands.)
Koag, old Koag!
O horrible insatiable mouth, that's why you laugh! You want
    to eat us all...all. You won't get away with it! Koag!
(Old Koag appears. The Old Man hides his bloodied hands behind him.)
My grandson, hurry!
(Koag moves toward the center door. The Old Man turns to Buddha.)
Not him! Him you won't eat! Koag!
(The slave returns.)
Softly, gently, Koag, don't wake him, he's sleeping. And wrap
    him well so he won't catch cold.
(The slave leaves. The Old Man to Buddha:)
No, no, don't laugh, you won't eat him!
Ah, ah, if only this were a dream and I would waken,
Oh, but I think — Buddha, help me! — I think this is real!
(Raises his hands, looks at the blood, tastes it with his tongue and lets out a cry.)
Oh, I see it's real! This isn't paint, it's my own salty, warm
    blood...
(Koag returns holding the baby.)
Is he sleeping?

OLD KOAG   He's sleeping, Master, he's sleeping —

OLD MAN   *(Leans over and admires his grandson.)*
O miracle, O immortal miracle of ill-fated man. I have no
other hope, Koag, my loyal slave, I have no other hope...

OLD KOAG   I know, Master; command me.

OLD MAN   Listen, Koag, bend over, listen to this secret: We're all lost
here — the Yangtze will eat us all...Be quiet, I can't leave;
I'm a Nobleman, I can't desert my people. But you, Koag,
you are a slave; for you it's not disgraceful to run from
danger,

Go! Take my grandson and go! There's still time.
Go far from the river, take our sturdiest cart,
Harness our strongest oxen, be off! Don't stop anywhere, go!
Hold him tightly in your arms, faithful slave; of all the
dreadful clan of Chiang, he alone remains. The clan of
Chiang has no other seed. If he's lost, we're all lost, and
the Dead will die.
Who will give them immortal water to drink by bearing them
a new grandchild? It will be gone, gone! The clan of
Chiang will sink into deepest shame — into Oblivion.
Is it dawn, Old Koag? Has the Morning Star melted away?

OLD KOAG   The sky hasn't a single star, Master, it's raining...raining.

OLD MAN   Louder! This river has deafened me, I don't hear very well.
(Points to Buddha.)
Do you hear his laughter?

OLD KOAG   *(Loudly.)*
Clouds! It's raining!

OLD MAN   Ah! Ah!
(Groans, paces back and forth.)
Shut the window so I won't hear it.
(Old Koag shuts the window.)
Come here, take the keys from my belt, Koag, open the
large chest, take all the gold and go! Take the five noble
treasures of the Chiangs,
The castellated ruby, the red sword, the gold ring, the ivory
staff of authority and the holy, yellow banner with the
green dragon!
Take them and go; they're his. Give them to him when he's
grown up; they're his.
Koag, eh Koag, raise him well, wild and proud; raise him not
to hoard his riches but to scatter them; that's the meaning
of nobility. Not to hoard one's youth but to scatter it;
that's what youth means. To hope for nothing from the
gods, do you hear? Nothing! Tell him that's what his
grandfather orders: to hope for nothing from the gods.
(Pauses a moment, hesitates, then makes a decision.)
Nor from the Ancestors!
(Old Koag steps back in fear.)
Why do you tremble? You don't dare repeat the words

90

I've commanded?

OLD KOAG　　Forgive me, I'm a slave, such words suit a nobleman, Master, not me.

I'm a slave, huddling under the feet of Buddha.

OLD MAN　　I wasn't speaking to you, I was speaking to my grandson. Tell him to keep courage in his heart,

Nothing else exists in this world but the heart of man, neither gods nor demons. You hear, Koag?

Tell him he has my blessing, and to return to our soil, here, not elsewhere, to build our Tower again on the same foundations, to cast roots in our soil again,

To marry and bear sons. Wild and good and noble and honorable is the clan of Chiang; it must not vanish from the earth.

If it is lost, the world will be poorer, a brilliant beast will be missing from God's jungle — the tiger. Do you hear, Koag?

OLD KOAG　　I hear, Master...

OLD MAN　　Go now. In your hands, my faithful slave, I entrust these almighty few pounds of flesh.

Wait, don't rush; let me bid him farewell.

(He bends over, looks at the child, then draws back.)

No, no, I mustn't wake him. Wrap him tightly so he won't catch cold...Go, and tell your doe-eyed son to come. I want him.

(Sobs are heard behind him. Li-Liang had come from the murdered man's room and was listening. The Old Man turns to her.)

Li-Liang, my child, do you want to go with him?

(Staggering, Li-Liang approaches. She looks at the baby, kisses the sheet on which it is wrapped, and shakes her head.)

LI-LIANG　　No, father —

OLD MAN　　Go, Koag. Goodbye. Goodbye.

(Koag leaves. The Old Man turns to the panoplies.)

Ancestors, famished spirits, you saw, you heard, we have no other hope. Dismount from the river, surround his cart, push the wheels so they won't sink in the mud, goad the oxen so they will run.

Spread yourselves across my grandson so he won't get wet;
wrap yourselves around him so he won't be cold! He's the
last Chiang, there is no other. I did all I could to save him.

But I am human, my power reaches only to the tips of my
fingers. O almighty dead, I surrender my grandson into
your hands.

(Climbs the three steps, stands and looks at Buddha.)

Buddha, Buddha, I ask only one thing of you — don't extend
a hand to strike him; let the Ancestors alone.

Yes, yes, everything's but wind and mist and a wink of the
eye; everything, everything; only my grandson here is real
flesh; don't touch him!

*(Turns, looks at Li-Liang who is also kneeling before the
statue of Buddha.)*

Li-Liang, my child, life is poison, poison —

LI-LIANG   It doesn't matter, father, death is sweet.

OLD MAN   Do you know how great my pain is, my child?

LI-LIANG   Yes.

OLD MAN   And you would give me your hand?

*(Li-Liang offers him her hand, weeping. The Old Man steps
back.)*

No, no, I can't touch it; look at my hands...Forgive me!

Don't! Be quiet! Don't say anything...to say No is a heavy
burden, and to say Yes, also. Be quiet!

May life be cursed! I raise my two bloodied hands: may life
be cursed!

YOUNG KOAG   *(Enters from the center door, bows.)*
Master, command me!

OLD MAN   Koag, go down to the courtyard, ring the large bell, call the
people to the Tower. Today is a great day; I want to talk
to them.

And take out the great uniform from the chest, the uniform I
wore when my son was born, the one I shall wear on the
day I die —

Take out the swords, the feathers, the rubies — and I shall
come that you may dress me.

(Koag leaves.)

This is a difficult moment, hold fast, old Chiang!

(Leaves from the center door.)

LI-LIANG   *(Kisses the earth.)*

Goodbye, my beloved, bloodied, tormented country, O
    China! Farewell...

(Picks up the bread that had fallen from the tray and kisses it.)

Goodbye, holy, salty bread of man; I bow and worship your
    power — farewell!

My child, my very being, my blood became milk to nourish
    you; I was born in this world for you, and now...farewell!

*(Looks around her, dazed; drags herself toward the threshold
of the murdered man's room.)*

Why this pain? Why this hatred? Why this bloodshed? How
    long? O terrible, inhuman laws! I struggle, I try hard, I
    can't understand them. They pass through my heart and
    crush it; they pass through my brain and shatter it; if I
    raise my eyes to see them, I am blinded.

I bow my head and obey. I obey, there's nothing more I
    can do. Our laws are beasts, hungry lions and tigers and
    wolves — who will save us Buddha, who?

(As though listening.)

Yes, yes — Death! Death! The cool door — you open it and
    leave.

(Bows before the low door.)

My husband, who will prepare tea for you below the earth?

I'm coming! I'm coming! Who will prepare hot water for you
    in winter, your clean, cool shirt in summer? I'm coming!
    I'm coming!

With you in life and in death; I place my hand in yours — let
    us go!

Ah, one moment, my beloved, while I comb my hair and
    adorn myself, while I perfume my breast. I'm coming.

*(Opens the chest, takes out her small mirror, her comb, her
perfume, her rouge. Softly sings a song much like a dirge.)*

"Three sentries did I post for you, my dear, for your sweet
    sake..."

*(Combs her hair swiftly, applies the cosmetics, singing softly
as the music accompanies her mournfully.)*

"I placed the sun among the mountains, the eagle in all
    valleys,

And the North wind, the cool North Wind, I placed in every

93

vessel..."
(Mei-Ling enters from the center door, hears the dirge and stops, startled. She motions the musicians to cease, and the music stops abruptly. Li-Liang sees Mei-Ling.)

MEI-LING   *(Sarcastically, with disdain.)*
Why are you wailing, sister?

LI-LIANG   *(Raising her head proudly.)*
I'm not wailing; I'm singing. I'm getting married tonight.

MEI-LING   *(Mockingly.)*
You're getting married tonight? Your eyes have grown wild; what's wrong, Li-Liang?

LI-LIANG   I won! I won!

MEI-LING   What? Who?

LI-LIANG   I won! I won! Don't ask!
(The loud ringing of the tower bell is heard.)

MEI-LING   The danger bell! Who ordered it to be rung?

LI-LIANG   Father. He's calling the people and the guests to come; I'm being married tonight.

MEI-LING   Come to your senses, Li-Liang, and listen to me, it's important: I had a terrible dream...

LI-LIANG   *(Smiles bitterly.)*
A dream? Just a dream? I spread out my hand and it fills with blood...

MEI-LING   Just now, at dawn...I don't believe in dreams, but this one frightened me...

LI-LIANG   *(Tired, quietly.)*
What dream?

MEI-LING   *(Softly.)*
Is he sleeping?

LI-LIANG   Yes...Yes...

MEI-LING   It seems our old father was sitting under a blossoming plum tree. He was holding a pipe, smoking, looking at the sky and admiring a white dove flying...

Suddenly a scream was heard and a hawk pounced but missed
and caught its beak in the earth.

In a frenzy it rushed at the dove again, but the dove hid
against father's chest.

"Give me the dove!" the hawk shrieked, "It's mine!"

"Don't you pity it?" father asked, and held the white bird
tightly in his arms.

"Why should I pity it?" replied the hawk angrily, "I do my
duty; I eat flesh; I was born for this."

"You are a cruel, merciless creature," said the Old Man, "and
God, one day..."

"What?" screamed the hawk, "What God? It's He who created
me like this. If He wanted to, He would have created me
to eat grass too, and I wouldn't be molesting living things.
But He made me a hawk. Give me the dove!"

The Old Man bared his arm. "Here, eat of my flesh, gorge
yourself, but let the dove be..."

The hawk swooped down, hooked itself onto the arm and
began to eat. It ate the one arm, it ate the other, then
jumped on the chest. "When you've had enough," the
Old Man whispered now and then, "when you've had
enough, stop."

But the hawk never had enough! It ate the chest, it ate the
shoulders, it ate the legs, it ate and ate...

Finally, all that was left was the head. It grabbed this in its
claws and flew away.

LI-LIANG   And the dove?

MEI-LING   It flew away — I don't know what happened to it.

LI-LIANG   I know, sister.

MEI-LING   Did you see the same dream, the same dream, Li-Liang?

LI-LIANG   I saw a white dove flying in my dream...and suddenly a hawk
pounced upon it...It must have been the same hawk,
Mei-Ling, the same, the same,
And it was not yet satiated.
(*She paints her lips, her eyebrows, singing the dirge softly.*)
"But O my darling, the sun has set, the eagle has fallen asleep,
And the North Wind, the cool North Wind, was taken by
every vessel..."

95

MEI-LING   Your mind is elsewhere, Li-Liang, the world is falling apart, and you have enslaved your mind to the bedroom and the soles of your son's feet.

LI-LIANG   You, Mei-Ling, have no husband, no son, no roots; all you have are wings,
Only the misfortune of wings and freedom.

MEI-LING   Don't shake your head. My road is long; it stretches thousands of miles, to the ends of China. And on that road only two walk, side by side, and they don't want a third —
My brother and I!
And now, we must go, there's much work ahead of us — to fetter the river. I've come to wake him; I've saddled the horses, we're off!

LI-LIANG   Won't you leave him with me for a few minutes, Mei-Ling? He's my husband, the father of my son.

MEI-LING   No!

LI-LIANG   *(Startled, shows her the low door.)*
Go, take him!
(Mei-Ling slowly opens the low door, afraid of startling her brother, and enters. The bell is heard again.)
Ah, Ah, there's nothing sweeter than death...
Thank you, my husband; you've taught me to love life and to love death!
(Suddenly a harrowing cry is heard. The low door opens, Mei-Ling rushes out and seizes Li-Liang.)

MEI-LING   Who?...Who? The Old Man?
(Li-Liang bows her head.)
And you, why didn't you call for help?

LI-LIANG   From whom? Help from whom, Mei-Ling?

MEI-LING   *(Grabs the mirror, smashes it into a thousand pieces.)*
May your face smash into a thousand pieces, too.
(Breaks the comb and the perfumes.)
Ah! So that's why you were dressing yourself like a bride; that's why your eyes shoot flames!
(Points to Buddha.)

96

You planned it with him; you took him from me!

LI-LIANG   Now he's mine, eternally! Why are you shouting? I'm his wife;
I'm going with him. *I*, not you.
I've won!
*(Opens the chest as she speaks, selects a scarf, checks it to
see if it's strong, wraps it around her neck, then turns to the
canary that has begun to warble.)*
Farewell, my canary!
(Bows to Mei-Ling.)
Farewell, my little sister...

MEI-LING   Where are you going?

LI-LIANG   I've saddled the horses, we're leaving!
*(Climbs the three steps, closes the curtain. For some time a
savage and mournful music plays. Mei-Ling bends down and
grasps the bloodied knife. The curtain opens and we see
Li-Liang fallen at Buddha's feet. The Old Man appears dressed
in his official uniform. He does not see Li-Liang and he does
not see Mei-Ling who has flattened herself up against the wall
under the panoplies. He raises his fist angrily at Buddha.)*

OLD MAN   Shame, shame on you. It's I shouting, old man Chiang!
What shame that God should condescend to play
With man's dread and danger!
You may be a lion, perhaps; but know this:
I'm not a lamb to stretch out my neck for slaughter!
You can do one thing only: you can kill me. Kill me, then!
But before I die I will let out a cry, Buddha,
I will let out a cry...
*(Bursts into sobs, descends the three steps, and walks toward
the outer door. Mei-Ling shows herself suddenly, hiding the
knife behind her back. The Old Man pauses, then stretches
out his hand.)*
My child, forgive me, it had to be — it had to be done, to
save the people. Yes, ask the Ancestors, too! They thrust
the knife into my fist...
*(Mei-Ling paces back and forth silently. The Old Man watches
in agony.)*
Ah, she's still young, she doesn't understand!
I bend before you, Mei-Ling, forgive me — Do you hear? I, I
who stand erect when I speak with God and listen to His

97

words and answer back – I, whom no one ever saw with
bent head – not God nor man, nor beast of the forest,
I, I, Old Chiang, bend before you, O inexperienced, dream-
ridden woman, and I beg of you: Forgive me!
(Waits, then suddenly, with fury:)
No? No? Don't set my blood boiling! Don't open the trap
door inside me for the demons to fly out!
I will plunge the knife into your heart, too! Why don't you
speak? Why don't you scream out your blasphemies?
(Mei-Ling paces back and forth, slowly smearing her brother's
blood on her face.)
Mei-Ling, I can't endure your silence, speak!
No, no, I don't regret it; you'll not see me cry again; look
at me! He's a real man who steps into water and does not
get wet, into fire and does not get burned, into death and
does not cry.
(Touches his eyes with his finger, then takes them away.)
There, dry!
(Mei-Ling clasps the knife tightly, raises it slowly and
approaches the Old Man. He bows his head quietly and
stretches out his neck. Savage music, then silence for some
time.)
I'm waiting. Why are you taking so long? Strike!
(Mei-Ling throws away the knife. The Old Man lifts his
head and sighs.)
Gone...gone...Chiang's generation has become weakhearted.
Chiang's generation cannot kill anymore.
(Young Koag opens the large door at left. The loud clamor of
the people is heard, shouts and weeping.)
What are those voices? No one shouts before the Master's
Tower.

YOUNG KOAG   It's the people; you've invited them, Lord; they're coming.
The old men lead the way with their staffs; behind come
weeping women carrying honey wrapped in green leaves to
sweeten Buddha; and in the center are the men, shouting.

OLD MAN   Open the doors of the Tower, put the people in the courtyard
and bring the chiefs, the men and the women before me. I
have something of great importance to tell them, news of
dreadful import. Go!
(Young Koag leaves.)

Bloodthirsty, many-headed beast, now you will drink my
blood, you will eat my flesh, and be satisfied!

I sit on my ancestral throne, on my tiger skin, and I wait...
The people give their accounting to the nobles, the nobles
to God, and God to no one. This is what order means!
But now, alas,

God gives an accounting to the nobles, the nobles to the
people, and the people to no one!

These new demons that will devour the world were brought
by the Westerners, a curse on them!

*(The large door opens, the people enter shouting and weeping
— the old men ahead, the women behind.)*

Don't all shout at once, I can't hear! Put your complaints into
some order; speak one by one!

(To the Mandarin.)

Speak, wise old man. Come close, don't tremble, I won't eat
you. You're a scribe, you sit in the marketplace with your
paper and ink — and your ears are large, like Buddha's; they
cover the marketplace, the city, all of China; you hear
everything and you write it down, scratch, scratch,
scratching the soul of man.

Speak, what did you hear in the marketplace? Don't tremble
I say; speak, what do the people want?

MANDARIN   Master, if you cut up a difficult deed, you'll see that it is
made up of thousands of little ones; it's then easy to act.

If you cut up an easy thought, you'll see that it's made up of
thousands of difficult ones; it's difficult, Master, for a man
to think and to speak his thoughts.

OLD MAN   *(Angrily.)*

Is that the meaning of wisdom? Is wisdom then a cuttlefish
that squirts its ink and clouds the water? Why don't you
speak as honestly, as simply, as straightforwardly as one
tosses a spear?

MANDARIN   I'm afraid, Master, I'm afraid...What I have to say is difficult,
I can't find the words. And if I did find them, I don't
have the strength to reveal them to you, Master; and if I
did have the strength,

I don't want to, I don't want to, Master, because I pity you...

OLD MAN   You pity *me?* You? Pity *me?*

99

(*Fearfully.*)
So, I've been reduced to this!

MANDARIN Master, I don't want to remain silent; necessity prods me. I don't want to speak; I'm afraid. What shall I do?

OLD MAN Don't speak, don't remain silent, you wretched man. Write! That's your job, old penpusher — a sly, cowardly job for slaves, for eunuchs and monks like you! Get out of my sight!
(*Turns to an old peasant.*)
Speak, peasant! You're not a wise man; your mind is not a ball of thin tangled threads;
It's an axe and it slashes! Slash, then!

PEASANT Nobleman, the old river has grown savage; it mounts the villages, drags behind it a long trail of sheep, oxen, dogs, people, carcasses. It eats, it eats, it eats, Master, but it is never satiated...
We fall on our faces to the earth, and we hear it shout;
"I want! I want! I want!" It shouts, and keeps descending.

OLD MAN What does it want?
(*To the Mandarin who is about to speak.*)
You, be quiet!
(*To the peasant.*)
What does it want?

PEASANT (*Quietly, slowly.*)
Your son!
(*A clamor rises from the people as they all step back with fear and stare at the Old Man. The Peasant remains alone in front of the Old Man, motionless. The Old Man closes his eyes and breathes deeply. Music is heard.*)

OLD MAN What did you say, old peasant?

PEASANT Your son, Nobleman. It's your son the River wants. Your son!
(*The agitated people look toward the door, to leave. The Old Man opens his eyes.*)

OLD MAN Silence! Silence!
(*To Young Koag.*)
It's getting dark; light the lanterns, Koag, open the window so

they can see me. This is a great moment, it needs light.
Don't shout; be quiet! Let the men stand to the right, the
   women to the left,
(Points to Buddha.)
And God in the center. I will speak!
For a hundred years I ate, I drank, I dressed, I made merry, I
   sat down at the sumptuous table of China —
And I paid nothing;
I was a nobleman, an idle drone, eating alone, drinking alone,
   reveling alone. I made no honey — I ate honey, and I paid
   nothing!
I've accumulated a large bill — one hundred years of
   sumptuous living — but now I must pay. Look!
(He raises his bloodied hands which were hidden inside his
wide sleeves.)

PEOPLE   Blood! Blood!

OLD MAN   This morning at dawn, God brought me the bill and I paid! I
               took out my heart, that great purse, and I paid!
            Look, I did not wash my hands so you could see. Look!
            (With a harrowing cry.)
            My son's!

MANDARIN   (Raises his hands in despair.)
            Your son's? In vain, in vain, you wretched man, in vain!

OLD MAN   What? What did you say? I can't hear.

MANDARIN   Nothing! What more can I say? Nothing!

OLD MAN   My son! I gave it my son! It ate, it ate, but it never had
               enough. Peasants and horses were not enough to satisfy it.
               So I cut out and gave it my entrails.
            Is it satisfied? Is it not? Why is it still shouting? My mind
               shakes.

MEN   Immortal is the Dynasty of Chiang, it comes out of the loins
               of Buddha. During great joys, it's not sorry to take a
               double portion; during great tragedies, it's not afraid to
               take a double portion.
            I bow in veneration, Master. You've taken all our suffering
               upon yourself.
            We've escaped! We're saved! Your son wanted to let loose the

101

terrible tiger, Freedom, into our homes and hearts, to eat
us. We're saved!

The river will calm down again. God will go back into his
sheath; our little life will turn green on the earth again.

OLD MAN   *(Looking at his hands.)*
Only I and these hands of mine know that happiness does
not exist...
(Suddenly grows fierce.)
Be quiet, leave me! I don't want to hear you any more!
Alas, is it then for these mouths, these bellies, these feet
and this mess of meat
That I've slaughtered a great soul?
(Rushes and grabs two or three peasants.)
Why are you living, you worm? And you, you frog? And
you, you monkey? Ah, ah, to save thousands of rats I've
killed a lion!
(Falls exhausted on his seat.)
Should I have done it or not? Ah, who's to tell me?

WOMEN   Don't be angry, Master, don't be sorry...You'll see, all the
fearsome powers will mellow. Here, we've gathered honey
in these green leaves to spread on the lips of Buddha;
We women have no other answer for gods or for men!

OLD MAN   Honey? Poor little people, he wants meat! Meat! Meat!
*(Alights from his seat, climbs the three steps, opens the
curtain.)*
Buddha, Buddha, this wretched people say they're bringing
you honey, do you hear? Honey to turn you sweet!
O dreadful lion...
*(Stops suddenly, terrified, for behind Buddha he sees Li-Liang
hanging by her scarf. He stumbles toward her. The people
gather behind him. The Old Man falls and kisses Li-Liang's
feet.)*
Beloved Li-Liang, you're gone...gone...I bow and worship
your feet. To our reunion, to our good reunion, my child...
*(The people are agitated, shouting. The Old Man turns
angrily.)*
Quiet! Li-Liang, my child, give my regards to the Ancestors.
Did I do my duty? Ask them, did I do my duty? I'm all
confused now. Goodbye! Farewell!

102

(He falls to the ground. Music. The Old Man raises his head, listens to the music, becomes tranquil and calls softly.)
Hu-Ming! Hu-Ming!

MAGICIAN   Command me, old Chiang, I'm here beside you.

OLD MAN   I'm in pain, Hu-Ming. Ease my pain, don't leave me! Are
all these things I see and hear and touch real? I won't have
it, Hu-Ming, I'm choking with anger.
Who made the world so narrow, Hu-Ming, so evil, so inferior
to the heart of man? I don't want it any more!
Hu-Ming, take me, alive, to the land of Myth. You are a
great craftsman; throw a silken bridal veil over the abyss.
Stitch it with red, with green, with yellow embroideries;
scatter suns on it, birds, gods, paradises, and console me.
Tell me that all is a dream, all is a dream, my son is a spring
cloud, and death — death is a strong, sweet fragrance that
makes us dizzy.
(He is overcome with sobs, then shakes himself in shame.)
I think of the Ancestors, I think of the Descendants, I think
of my race and pity it.
Hu-Ming!

MAGICIAN   At your command, Nobleman.

OLD MAN   Are you ready?

MAGICIAN   Ready! All those hours you struggled, entangled in the webs
of Necessity, I, free of sons, nobilities and old debts, have
been working.
I was shaping the world as you had ordered, old Chiang, wide
and deep enough to hold the heart of man.
I fitted Necessity with wings and turned it into freedom.
I raised hot winds that caused buds to swell and stumps and
heads to blossom.
I'm ready. Order them to light the incense burners, to scatter
intoxicating aromas that man's brain may sprout wings to
follow me.
Master, you no longer need intoxication; you have the largest
wing of all — Pain!
With your permission I shall tear down the boundaries of the
visible and the invisible, I shall abolish the world, I shall
cover the abyss with a veil. I shall begin!

103

OLD MAN   Onward! Hu-Ming, do what God had not the courage to do!
           Turn the wheel, put us in the unmoving center, in the axis,
           that we may admire the world moving.
           Give the reel a kick, wind and unwind the fairy tale!
           Hu-Ming, the heart of man is a tangled ball of caterpillars;
           blow on them and turn them into butterflies.

MAGICIAN   (Traces a circle again, puts the twelve signs of the zodiac in
           their places again, murmuring the name of each.)
           Cock — Hare — Tiger — Ape — Pig — Snake — Ox —
           Dragon — Dog — Sheep — Rat — Horse!
           (Slaves appear with censers and sprinkle the people with
           perfume. Music.)
           Keep order! Don't mix the living with the dead, freemen with
           the slaves, men with women, humans with animals.
           Vision is an army, it needs discipline.
           Here, in the first row, the spirits...Can't you see them? Good,
           then! If you saw them they would disappear. Behind the
           spirits, in the second row, the free peasants; further back
           the slaves, and then the house dogs, the oxen, the
           monkeys, the parrots...
           Where did we stop, my Nobleman, do you remember?

OLD MAN   I remember. Saripoutta's ox-cart had arrived filled with
           dancers, ascetics, monkeys.
           He stooped, Buddha stooped, I remember, like a black swan,
           he stooped over the waters and watched his image dying.
           And around him the visible and the invisible gathered, and
           waited.

MAGICIAN   Alas for you, Old Man, Buddha has not yet freed your
           memory, for you remember. Let me lean, then, a large
           ladder against the air, Master, that you may climb to the
           top level of truth where neither forgetfulness nor memory
           exist.
           Blood does not exist, nor water, nor tears, nor sweat; nothing
           exists! Nothing! I clap my hands and begin.
           (The Magician puts on the yellow mask of the Spirit, and
           immediately the set changes. Sweet, unworldly music is
           heard.)
           Take your places, animals, spirits, people! Make circles
           around the Holy Tree, and let each one stand according to

his rank in nature.

Animals, dark, indestructible roots of mankind,

(Claps his hands.)

Come! Come! Spirits, descend from the trees, ascend from the
waters, no one is watching you, come forth! And you,
people, sacks filled with blood, tears, urine and sweat,
come to purge yourselves.

And you, fellow-athletes, dancers, ascetics and monkeys,
shake loose from Buddha's ox-cart, scatter across the
threshing floor and plant the imagination with both fists.

These are the people, lost in their passions, drowned in
tears, caught in the web of Necessity. Pity them! Their
heads, their breasts, their loins are overstuffed with straw;
set them on fire, that they may shine; throw Buddha upon
them like burning coals.

Brother, my eyes are dazzled. Just as a king, overcome with
wine, grabs a large golden tray overbrimming with
emeralds, sapphires, turquoises and rubies, and tosses them
into his marble courtyard,

So did this ox-cart overbrim and scatter itself over the earth.

Women leap from the cart as copper bracelets jingle on their
feet and arms; gold coins weigh down their high, warring
breasts — my brother, the whole world is a woman dancing.

MANDARIN   Toss your heads, chase away the nightmare, my children.
They're casting spells over you; resist them! Don't let your
brains become blurred!

PEOPLE   Don't listen to the old sage; he's turned senile; Look! Look!
The dancers have hung their ornaments like offerings, and
the entire Holy Tree has sprouted with silver belts and red
sandals.

Look, the black slaves have set up a royal tent of heavy silken
velvet, and puffing and panting, are carrying the holy
instruments of the liturgy.

The threshing floor has filled with wooden masks; it has taken
on a voice and soul; it laughs and mourns, like a man, like
a woman.

This is not an ox-cart; it's a head, my brothers, the head of
Buddha — and it has opened.

Women and men bend in rows over the river, and before the
liturgy begins they bathe and comb their hair, paint

themselves, pour perfumes over their hair, their ears, their
armpits.

Saripoutta has freed himself at last from baths and perfumes;
from head to toe he's become spirit. He is standing in the
middle of the threshing floor and is offering a sacrifice.

He is offering for a sacrifice the shadow of a large yellow
parrot, the shadow of a large yellow parrot!

(*Music.*)

MAGICIAN   All sit cross-legged on the ground; be quiet! Open your
minds, people; shake the earth from your eyelashes, all of
you! Look:

The spirits of the wilderness approach with reverence,
trembling to hear the commands of the Mind.

PEOPLE   Brothers, the bones of my head are coming apart with great
joy! I see stones, unburdened of their weight, slowly
rising, uniting by themselves and fitting together like a
great thought...A Royal Palace, like a multi-colored mist,
rises noiselessly in the sun and shines at the river's edge.

Oh, in the large, marble courtyard the doors open wide and
I see a prince entering, standing tall in a silver carriage
drawn by four horses...

And in front, holding the red reins, a tall naked man towers
like a bronze god with a wide, golden belt around his loins.

The slaves run, but slowly the prince moves his hand and
turns his gaze upon us like a setting sun.

Ah! His eyes fill with tears as he looks at us.

Mogalana rises and stretches out his hands toward us.

MOGALANA   Be silent! Be silent! It's Buddha, my brothers, Buddha, in the
flower of his age, with his black, curly hair, with his
towering, impregnable brow.

Buddha speaks to Hanna, his slave.

BUDDHA   Hanna, faithful slave, a great cry split the air: "Buddha!"
That's the terrible name I heard, Hanna.

I was frightened, I covered my ears, and the voice issued
stronger and clearer from my entrails: "Buddha, rise, that
the world may rise. Waken that the world may waken!
Buddha, crop your curly hair, doff your royal, golden
clothing, desert your wife and your son! Buddha,

Set out for the forest, alone, without fire, without water,

without woman, without hope. Pity the trees and the birds, pity the beasts and the gods, pity mankind."

HANNA   O Lord...

BUDDHA   Hanna, my loyal slave, saddle Kantaka, my beloved horse, wrap his hoofs with velvet so they won't clatter on the stones, and wait at the outer door of the Palace;
I go to see my son's face and to bid my wife farewell.
Quiet now, don't cry, don't fall at my feet, Hanna; help me to save myself, to save us.

PEOPLE   Ah, my entrails are tearing apart, brother, as I abandon my son, my wife...For deep within me I feel it is I in another body who mourns and struggles to free himself from the world's web
And to shout the great "Farewell."
The whole world has grown lighter and sails under the moon, like a green cloud...O Buddha, like a crowned athlete returning to his country as breakwaters crumble to welcome him, O Buddha, tear down the ramparts of the flesh also.
Brothers, be silent! Hanna is returning, weeping, and he's bringing with him a pure white, slender horse.
Hanna is embracing it now, he's talking to it, as though it's a man, and both of them have broken out in lamentation.
Buddha has stretched out his hand, quietly, sweetly, pleadingly, and he's caressing it.

BUDDHA   Kantaka beloved, remember how I fed you from my palms, remember how I loved you like a brother, and what talks we had, the two of us, on our long rides.
And now, my brother, I'm asking you for a favor: Help me! Sprout wings, pass through the castle gates, trick my father's sentries so they won't see you, won't hear you, and take the path of the wilderness
That we may be saved. Kantaka, don't neigh angrily, don't refuse me. I shall leave.

HANNA   Master, they say that a wife's tears melt even the hardest stone; they say that a son's tears cause even stones to blossom,
Master, did you bid farewell to your revered wife and your son?

107

BUDDHA   Hanna, my son was resting at his mother's side, cuddled
          against her breast as though he were still unborn...I bent
          down to see his face, to take it with me as a consolation.
          But his mother had thrown her arm around him like a lioness
          and guarded the precious newborn head — and I left softly,
          lest I wake them...
          Faithful slave, I touch your knees; if ever I have spoken
          harshly to you, forgive me...I believed I was immortal, a
          brilliant thought that leapt from the head of Brahma.
          I thought all other men were but dust scattered by the feet of
          God as he walked upon the earth.
          Now, brother, I recognize you in the lightning flash of death;
          forgive me.

HANNA   Gautama, my prince, may you live for many years. I kiss
          your shoulders, I kiss your hands, I kiss your knees; let
          me go with you.

BUDDHA   Forgive me, my brother, I cannot. Alone, without a
          companion, I shall thrust into the dark, cool heart of the
          forest; the wilderness does not hold two, my brother.
          I take back my heart, Hanna, I tear it away from my beloved
          ones; I take back my eyes, Hanna, I take back my mind, I
          take back my entrails, I unsheath myself from the world —
          farewell.
          And you, Kantaka, my brother, I will leave you at the
          entrance to the forest. Kantaka, your eyes have brimmed
          with tears, they fall warm and heavy on my palms. Ah,
          the glance of an animal and its mute pleading!

TEMPTATION   Gautama, I will come with you.

BUDDHA   Who are you?

TEMPTATION   Mara, the spirit of Temptation; I am an ascetic too, you see,
          and I enjoy the wilderness.

BUDDHA   Come.

MOGALANA   An earthquake is destroying the foundations of the earth;
          the Palace has sunk into the pit of our minds; only one
          road remains and it shines endlessly;
          And Buddha, grasping the mane of his horse tightly, throws
          off hills and plains behind him and rides on.

Bearded, vociferous gods rise from ravines, descend from
mountain tops and, leaning on their knobby staffs, bend
to catch a glimpse of the rider.
"Is it Brahma or Vishnou, or can it be Siva, the indestructible
god who, without mercy, unites, gives birth and kills?
Who is it? Who is it?" the wild glens shout and echo.
A young man and a girl embracing under a tree break away
frightened; an old elephant turns its furrowed head, and its
face glitters like that of a man.
And the apelike god, Hanouman, finds his voice again in his
turbid brain and from a tall date tree shrieks his advice:
"Go straight ahead, Gautama, with my blessing!"
The savage mountain tops catch fire, the dawn is breaking,
the Morning Star hangs like dew from Buddha's curly hair,
And behold, an enormous Tree appears before him, without
leaves, without fruit, without shade;
And only at its peak, five long branches toss and beat in the
windless air and struggle to conquer their fate — to turn
into wings.
And now Buddha, Buddha — look at him, brothers — he
stops, jumps down to earth, waves his hand, and cries:
"Greetings, tall Tree of the struggle! Here where your deep
roots strive to become wings and to fly away, I will sit
cross-legged, and I swear:
I will not rise until Salvation is wedged here between my two
hands.
My loyal Kantaka, it's time for us to part; you've performed
your duty well, very well. If I am liberated, you will
become a white, immortal flame shining inside my mind."

PEOPLE   Ah, the great-spirited horse neighs mournfully and leans its
wet, steaming neck against Buddha's shoulder,
And then suddenly it falls lifeless to the ground.

MOGALANA   Buddha gently steps over the warm, beloved corpse, and
without turning to look, moves toward the desolate Tree
and sits cross-legged at its roots.
Silence! Silence! The great task of asceticism now begins;
motionless, with trunk erect like a pillar of fire,
Buddha glows under the tall fruitless and
flowerless Tree.

PEOPLE	Oh, he has sunk into ecstasy! His eyes have turned inward; the top of his head has risen like bread.
	What are those black shadows, what are those blue flashes of light that pass over him?
MOGALANA	They are the days and nights; they are the suns and the moons; they are the years.
PEOPLE	An arena of light spreads around him, an arena of light, seven arm-lengths wide.
MOGALANA	It's not an arena; Buddha is passing through the first cycle of his asceticism; motionless, with his eyes turned inwards, he sees the whole forest.
	He struggles, the sweat runs from his armpits; Buddha trembles like a snake floundering in the sun, coiling around rocks and struggling to shed its skin.
PEOPLE	The bright arena around him opens and widens; he sees mountains, rivers, cities and people in the translucent air.
MOGALANA	Buddha's reason opens and widens...It passes beyond the forest, it conquers India...Buddha's head fills with mountains and cities; swarms of men ascend from the furrows of his brain;
	They work, weep, kiss and then return into the furrows of his brain.
	Buddha cocks his ears and listens: Like a vast silk factory his country sprawls everywhere, and like silkworms the people crawl, opening and shutting their mouths voraciously —
	And standing over them, feeding them, is Buddha.
	Only he, in all the world, remains standing; he distributes forage to the people and waits.
	"Let them eat, let them eat," he thinks, "to complete the full cycle of the worm, to sprout wings and fly away."
PEOPLE	Buddha grows pale, he dissolves; his strength spills out and flows over the ground.
MOGALANA	He holds the infants of all of India to his breast and suckles them; he is the Father, he is the Mother, he is the Son of India.
	Approach with reverence and listen: He weeps like a baby in

its cradle; he laughs and quivers like a groom with his
bride; he sings like a woman in love at dusk behind a thick
lattice.

Now he falls silent and shudders—an earthquake erupts! A
city topples inside him, a wound opens and heals,
everything is lost...

The sun ascends, doors open and swarms of people pour out
over the soil; the sun descends, the black tide withdraws,
doors shut again, and the people disappear.

Buddha's breast opens and closes as though it were the door
of India.

PEOPLE   Brothers, Buddha is dancing! His numberless hands go up and
down, his numberless feet go up and down. Buddha is a
wheel of lightning flashes; I grow dizzy.

MOGALANA   Step back, people, or his wings will touch you! The ghosts
have been let loose, the chains have broken, the doors have
become unhinged, the land shakes to its foundations. Old
Man Time has become bewildered, Wisdom has gone mad
—Buddha is dancing!

The sun rushes headlong, dawn and dusk have merged,
noonday has vanished. The moon flashes in the sky like a
sickle; the eye has barely time to see it before it swells,
becomes a breast full of milk, then pours out its milk,
deflates, becomes a sickle again, becomes a silver thread
and dissolves in the air.

Winter has fallen, the earth has grown barren; Buddha turns
his eyes, and at once grass spreads over the spring plains,
and the trees blossom; he turns his eyes again, and the
leaves wither, the fruit rots, the snow falls.

The weather and the land get drunk; Mind, that hoarder,
opens his chests and scatters gold coins and precious
stones he has treasured with such miserliness as he dug and
sifted the sky and the earth...Buddha opens and shuts his
eyes and the universe lights up and darkens.

PEOPLE   Help, Mogalana! I see fiery horsemen rushing upon me! Help
me!

MOGALANA   They're not horsemen, don't be afraid, brothers; they are the
thoughts of Buddha.

111

PEOPLE   I see beggars now, Mogalana, with saffron robes, with
           begging bowls — and I, too, am happy to give a piece of
           bread as charity — my soul.

MOGALANA   They're not beggars in saffron robes; they are the thoughts
           of Buddha.
           He thinks: "I want to conquer the world!" He frowns and
           says: "I will unleash armies, I will burn cities, I will rush
           down like a horseman with his spear and slaughter the
           earth; I am War!"
           And then, immediately after, he thinks, serene in the coolness
           of his mind: "I will find a filling and simple word, and I
           will divide it among all begging bowls that the people may
           be satiated; I am not War, I am Buddha!"

PEOPLE   Oh! Oh! A gnome, a sly black boy leaps and crouches before
           him. I'm afraid!

MOGALANA   Don't be afraid, don't be afraid! It's his faithful companion,
           the brave upholder of the ascetic, the thrice-enchanting
           hermit, Temptation!
           He's arrived, brothers, Temptation, the black Buddha, the
           black touchstone of man's trial has arrived; he will rub
           himself now against yellow Buddha,
           To see, it's said, if Buddha is in truth pure gold.

TEMPTATION Gautama, eh, Gautama! He does not hear…His head has
           stiffened; his unmoving eyes have thickened and glazed; his
           nostrils, his ears, his lips are blocked with soil — Gautama!
           Alas, the curly hair of your youth has fallen, your skin is
           flaking away and rotting; your breath stinks, your spine
           scatters like a broken rosary,
           And your holy royal head has shriveled like a gourd and
           hangs in the air, Gautama.
           The owls were fooled, they took you for a hollow tree and
           laid their babies in your belly; and the small sparrow, the
           skylark, the green linnet, the chaffinch, have uprooted your
           beard to build their nests…
           All winter, buried beneath the rotted weeds, you hissed and
           panted like a turtle; all summer you barked like a dog,
           howled like a wolf, slunk through graveyards like a jackal
           and dug up the dead.
           You dug up dead people, you dug up dead times and thoughts

112

and played with their bones;
Your brains preened with pride, you sat cross-legged in the
center of the earth, motionless, and the entire Universe —
stones, people, stars, ideas — whirled, whirled and whirled
around you.
But now, unplug your ears from the weeds and soil and
listen to the message I bring you: Gautama, the gods
promenade you through the sky and howl with laughter:
Listen to what I heard Siva shouting last night as he laughed:
"Gautama seems to me like a shameless over-trained monkey;
I will stretch out my hand, seize him by the throat and toss
him into my courtyard.
The little red-assed monkey who once played there has died;
its chain lies empty. I will tie up Gautama in its stead!"

BUDDHA   Who shouted this?

TEMPTATION   Siva.

BUDDHA   Who?

TEMPTATION   Siva!

BUDDHA   Mind, thrust these words of the god Siva deeply inside you
like a knife. Memory, famished hyena, rise, seize these
words of the god Siva like meat!
Who laughed? Why do you laugh?

TEMPTATION   Aha! Gautama has still not conquered anger and pride!
You have devastated your body in vain, your mind has
shaken the universe in vain; Gautama has still not
conquered Gautama!

PEOPLE   Buddha falls prone on the earth in shame!
The whole sky above him laughs and mocks!
Be quiet; Hanna, his faithful slave, appears again on horseback.
He dismounts, holds a long sword in his hand and hurriedly,
panting, approaches Buddha.
He bares his right shoulder, he opens his mouth.

HANNA   Gautama, my prince, may you live for many years. Get up!
Enemies have set foot on your parents' Palace; your old father
lies on the threshold, drowned in blood; your faithful
slaves are lying around him, their warm corpses are still
steaming and the flames are devouring your rich cellars.

Get up, Gautama, take up arms and let your horses' hoofs
shoot sparks again on your country's stones.
Don't you recognize me, Lord? I am Hanna, Hanna, your
faithful slave.

BUDDHA   I hear a beloved voice and weeping in the wind...Who calls
me? I heard my name.

HANNA   Your son calls you, Lord, your son and your revered wife...
There, look at them: their arms tied behind their backs,
blood-spattered and half-naked, they are dragged off to
slavery by their mocking conquerors.
Rise! I bring you your father's sword, Gautama, and your
faithful horse, Kantaka...Ah, you've recognized him, Lord,
you shake the earth from your body, and he paws the
ground and neighs with joy.

BUDDHA   Faithful, beloved companion, my brother Kantaka, how glad I
am to see you.

HANNA   Lord, my Lord, rise up! Do not seek liberation in the
wilderness. Leave the shadows, seize flesh, and knead. The
world is not made of thoughts, sighs and visions; it's made
of stones and waters and people.
Rise up and take your post in the battle!

BUDDHA   Enough! Give me the sword; my heart leaps like a tiger.

HANNA   Take it!

BUDDHA   Aaah!

PEOPLE   The sword was made of air and it disappeared!
The faithful slave disappeared too, he became but swirling
smoke in the air; and the horse was but white mist that
scattered.
Buddha grovels on the earth and weeps.
Hunched and crouching like a dog that bit his master,
Temptation lurks behind the tree and trembles.
Buddha rises and looks sadly around him.

BUDDHA   Mara...Mara...don't be afraid, come closer...I realized too
late that you were Temptation; but your words, filled with
bitterness and meaning, shook my heart...
Yes, yes, there still remains a lump of mud inside me, warm

114

and beloved mud that does not want to be freed, to become spirit and to scatter...

And inside this lump of mud are three famished sprouts — Father, Son, Country —

That have not yet understood the secret, and struggle to blossom.

Love, duty, hope, I blow upon you, scatter!

PEOPLE   Ah, my eyes can no longer look upon his agony. Buddha has drowned in the soil and the weeds, his flesh has thickened and hardened like a turtle shell; smoke rises from his holy head.

He's rolling now over a mountain of skulls, searching among them, biting them, climbing up and down and growling over the bones like a hungry dog.

He barks, laughs, wears the skulls, in a wild intoxication, and each skull is different.

Look, like a bird now, he dances, bends and pecks the earth with a beak as large as a pelican's as though searching for worms to eat.

Now, like a rhineroceros, he tramples the earth and with erect horn jabs at the skulls and tumbles them down.

Ah, there he is, changing masks again; he lifts himself up like an ape and tries to stand on his hind legs, to see. To see what? The man of the future!

MOGALANA   Silence, people! Lightning slashes his brain; Buddha struggles to remember.

He's going through the darkest, most difficult struggle. His mind has surpassed the boundaries of India; it has taken up the whole earth — the whole sphere of the world has become his head.

These are his skulls, these, that in numberless lives Buddha filled with eyes, with teeth, with brains; he filled them with trees, sky, women and ideas.

And now he struggles to remember the bodies he passed through; what animal he was, what god he was before he walked the earth wearing his final skull — the skull of Gautama.

For thousands of years he has lived, barked, howled, neighed, chirped; for thousands of years he has glittered like a god, become a woman, become a man, killed, loved, sinned,

115

died, returned to earth again, loved more, sinned less, understood all, until he became Gautama.

And now, look at him with terror; he's struggling to stop at last the wheel of birth, to pour out his body and his soul into the earth, to empty himself of animal, god, and man — to become flame and to die out.

PEOPLE   The earth and sky seem an egg to me, and inside it like a yolk, is the sun, and in the sun there's a bird — Buddha!
And it pecks the shell with its beak to break it and leave.

MOGALANA   A Drone is Buddha, my brothers, a large Drone. In spring when the thyme blossoms on the mountains, and the Queen Bee sighs in her fragrant beehive, she begins to feel constrained, stretches her wings, tries them out, licks her belly and prepares herself.

A large Drone is Buddha as he shines in the sun and wears the great panoply of Eros.

His sight intensifies — his unmoving eye governs the entire dome of the sky, he holds the East and West, the North and South like four multi-colored kites;

His hearing intensifies — he hears the Queen adorning herself, he hears her lady friends, her bridal maids, buzzing around her, encouraging, advising and pushing the bride out of her waxen home;

His taste intensifies — he tastes all the wells and all the roots; he pillages souls as though they were honey-cakes; his tongue flicks between earth and sky like a knife harvesting honey, and eats;

His smell intensifies — he smells the fragrant bridal body in the wind, and secret messages descend into his loins;

His touch intensifies — beneath his joyous belly he feels the downy body of the Queen nestling and filling;

His mind intensifies — like a male octopus it spreads, slowly caresses and squeezes life, that female octopus, in its multi-mouthed tentacles.

Buddha has put on the great panoply of Eros and the whole earth has become a Bee-Mother.

PEOPLE   He doesn't bark any more, he doesn't laugh, he doesn't cry, he doesn't fast, he doesn't struggle. He has reached the peak of endeavor and entered the smooth road of

116

liberation.

Bathing is no longer a temptation, food now nourishes his
soul only; sadness, joy, sleep, wakening, speech, silence,
all serve their master.

And Mara too, has become a lance, a faithful lance that
shines among the armies of Buddha's head.

Underneath the stars, throughout the whole earth I can
distinguish only Buddha's head shining like a midnight sun.

Help, Mogalana! What is this miracle I see? The air has filled
with wings.

MOGALANA Open your eyes, brothers, close your mouths; the gods are
descending.

How do scorpions leap and thrash and writhe on the lighted
hearth? So do the gods — look at them! They leap, thrash
and writhe inside the fiery head of Buddha.

PEOPLE Buddha leans on the dry Tree and oh, miracle, the withered
Tree fills with blossoms. They fall slowly, thickly, on his
hair, his shoulder, his chest —

And they cover Buddha!

Ah, how slowly, how serenely does salvation fall, like
flowers, like tufts of snow that cover the earth.

Salvation sits like a baby nine months old wrapped in
Buddha's entrails, and all his veins, blood and thoughts
bestir themselves to feed it.

Oh, Buddha is rising now, brothers, and the whole world
with its mountains, waters and ideas rises with him.

Saripoutta has moved, he has spread out his right hand,
drawn back the invisible reins and holds the bridle
tightly...

The spirits have set out too eagerly and now he orders them
to assemble, to turn back.

All faces have frozen, their eyes have clouded, their bodies
have emptied, they tremble in the air and vanish.

Ah, Saripoutta gathers the whole wealthy procession again
inside his high forehead.

Don't shout! Saripoutta has opened his arms and prays.

SARIPOUTTA Thank you, Mind, great nobleman of the imagination,
wealthy, dexterous and omnipotent Lord of Ceremonies.
You marshaled them all so well in the air, filled with flesh

117

and light, legend and truth.

You leaped out of my forehead, you played like a child
frisking on the foaming shore of the sea. You grasped the
sand and said:

"This is flesh, man and woman." You blew upon it and
immediately the flesh began to speak, to hurt, to want;

You blew again, and it ceased to exist.

You grasped a fistful of azure air and said: "This is Buddha"
— and inside the darkened heads of men flashed the youth,
the flight, the struggles and the liberation of Buddha. You
blew again, and Buddha vanished.

Like an eagle that snatches its weak-winged children on its
strong wings and sweeps them high to the wind's peak,

And with one forceful shake scatters them to the winds and
lets them fly as best they can,

So did you snatch all men also, and winnow them in the air.
Now set them down on earth again, cover their eyes with
earth again, and cut away the wings from their temples;
you've played well, but enough!

PEOPLE   How do the deceiving invisible powers play us on their
fingertips!

Ah, how do thirsting brains open to receive the miracle and
are still insatiable!

I see Mogalana and Saripoutta still embracing, cheek to cheek.

All during the time we tossed on the wind's peak, these two
did not even move.

And the ox-cart still stands covered, motionless, and the
buffaloes chew their food under the Holy Tree...

Only inside our temples did all this variegated fluttering
of wings explode.

BLOSSOMING   Buddha, Buddha, O azure wind, take me!
CHERRY TREE

VOICE OF THE   We're lost!
FIRST SENTRY   (The Old Man jolts upright, the people let out a cry, the
vision disappears. Muffled, troubled music. The door at the
left is forcefully opened, the Second Sentry enters panting,
covered with mud.)

SECOND SENTRY   Master, brothers, we are lost!

YOUNG KOAG	O Buddha, Buddha, do not pluck the red wings from my temples, do not take the wine from my lips, do not empty my arms.
BLOSSOMING CHERRY TREE	O miracle, O sweet caress of the wind, farewell!
MANDARIN	O Mind, I have sinned, forgive me; I did not know the imagination had so many secret joys and that, even above truth, the Myth shines As round and full of light as the full moon.
OLD MAN	*(To the Magician.)* Thank you Hu-Ming, you have filled my heart with cool shade; you took me to liberation by the quickest well-shaded path. *(To the Sentry.)* Why are you shouting? *(To the People.)* Don't listen to him, my children. He'll tell you that we enter a dark cave, stumble, slip and knock our heads on stalactites — but then suddenly an invisible hand thrusts a lighted torch in our fists and the whole cave is illuminated, our hearts grow steady again and we proceed in the glow without stumbling — The word of Buddha is like that lighted torch.
SECOND SENTRY	Master, I kiss your feet; bend your revered head, hear me.
OLD MAN	Who is this crude peasant who rips freedom's silken net? Rise, Buddha, Spider of the sky, and swaddle him That he may not stir, or shout, or resist; that this peasant, too, may enter into blessedness.
SECOND SENTRY	*(Touches the Old Man with fear, as though he wanted to wake him.)* Master...
OLD MAN	Who touched me? My eyes are blinded from too much light. Who are you?
SECOND SENTRY	Don't you recognize me, Master?
OLD MAN	How can I recognize you? All the boundaries have crumbled; I lay down to sleep, and dream I am a cloud; I wake, and

119

become a man.

Am I a cloud? Am I a man? What is sleep? What is awakening? I wonder, do I wake or am I being transformed? Or could both be true? Or both fantasy? Or nothing? The Nothing that fills the abyss?

O Buddha, Buddha, the mist unceasingly becomes a fortress and the fortress becomes mist. I look at it from the bottom level: it's a fortress; I look at it from the upper level: it's mist.

Ah, only now do I understand: the mist, only the mist is the impregnable fortress.

SECOND SENTRY   Don't rant, Master; wake up, listen to me, forget Buddha. Look at me!

OLD MAN   How can I forget him? He won't forget me; Buddha still hangs on my eyelids...Who are you?

SECOND SENTRY   The second river sentry, Master!

OLD MAN   What river?

SECOND SENTRY   What river! The Yangtze.

OLD MAN   Ah! The great mist thickens, it becomes solid, China is coming.

We enter the dream again, the other dream, the earthen one. See, there is our village, our fields, the road that ascends, the Tower.

Ah, welcome! Yes, yes, you are the second sentry; speak, I am ready.

(Points to the people.)

And all these with their saffron robes, they're ready, too... Well?

SECOND SENTRY   *(Shouting.)*

Master, the second dam has also fallen!

OLD MAN   *(Quietly.)*

Very well. The second dam has also fallen; is that all?

(Laughs mockingly.)

On a small star, on a narrow strip of land called China, on one footprint of earth, a water-worm swelled, a water-worm called Yangtze —

And it drowned a few miniscular ants called men that scurried back and forth in the mud.

120

	Is that all? Is that why the hairs on your head stand on end? Is that why you troubled to come, you thick-headed peasant, and have frightened away that great wing, the vision?
SECOND SENTRY	But Master, don't you understand the terrible news I bring? *(To the people.)* Brothers, the river broke the second dam, it's drowning the villages; corpses are descending to the sea layer on layer! Master...
OLD MAN	Very well, very well, why are you shouting? I'm not deaf.
SECOND SENTRY	Brothers, why are you waiting? Get up, let's leave! Grab your babies in your arms, make a bundle of your lives, load the old people on your backs and let's be off! At any moment now the river will break the third dam, the last one, and it will come here and drown us! *(Runs up and down through the people, shakes them as though to wake them.)*
PEOPLE	*(Frightened, they rub their eyes and yawn.)* I'm seeing a lovely dream, don't wake me! The Yangtze? What Yangtze?
SECOND SENTRY	Wake up, brothers, why do you look at me so foolishly? Blow that azure smoke, Buddha, from your brains! The Yangtze has broken the second barrier, too — we'll be lost! *(Pounds loudly on the low door at right.)* Chiang! Chiang! Chiang! *(The door opens, Mei-Ling comes out, pale, fierce, but restrained. Music.)* Mei-Ling, O fierce and stubborn lady, your brain has not clouded over; you see, you hear, you make decisions. The Yangtze has toppled the second barrier — save your people!
MEI-LING	*(To the Old Man, with hatred.)* Why don't you rise? Why don't you take command? Didn't you hear?
OLD MAN	I heard, Mei-Ling, I heard...The second barrier fell...more villages drowned...the Yangtze is coming. *(To the Sentry.)*

Isn't that what you said?

PEOPLE   *(Startled awake.)*
          Master, Old Chiang, let's leave! The Yangtze is coming!

OLD MAN   Let no one move! I want no tears; my eyes are filled too —
          I don't want our tears to mingle.
          (Points to the ancestral panoplies.)
          It's with these I have to settle accounts. Give way, make
          room!
          Eh, Ancestors, if you've tricked me, if blood has been spilled
          in vain, then watch out! I'll dig up your graves with my
          own nails, I'll toss your bones to the watermill, grind them
          into flour, I'll bake them into bread,
          I'll cast them to the dogs!

MEI-LING Let the Ancestors be, they're dead; look to the living,
          murderer Chiang,
          There's still time!

OLD MAN   I did all I could, more than I could; don't shout!
          I'm tired, I'm disgusted! Enough! I've made all the gestures of
          a man fighting...I've spoken all the brave, proud words a
          nobleman should say...I've pleaded, threatened, killed, like
          a nobleman.
          I'm drained out, I'm drained out, Mei-Ling, and now I make
          the final, the wisest gesture of man: I cross my hands.
          I cross my hands, Mei-Ling; I close my mouth; I hold my
          head high, and wait. What am I waiting for? I don't know.
          I wait.
          (To the Mandarin.)
          What are you muttering?
          (To the People.)
          And you, what are you shouting? Poor, wretched people!
          They still want to resist. So you still don't understand?
          Was it in vain then, withered leaves of the plane tree, was
          it in vain that the autumn wind of Buddha blew upon you?
          (To the Mandarin.)
          Are you still muttering, you old ruin? Haven't the words run
          dry in your throat yet, you old gossiper? If you have
          something to say, say it openly before my people.

MANDARIN *(Slowly.)*

122

Master...Master...In vain, in vain, in vain you killed your son...In vain...
(Mei-Ling comes closer to hear; the Old Man shakes with fear.)

OLD MAN   Are my ears buzzing? Stop, Earth, that I may hear. Come closer, you old ruin; what did you say? In vain?

MANDARIN   Master...

OLD MAN   Go on! Strike, then; don't be afraid!

MANDARIN   The river did not want your son...It was useless! Useless! You killed him for nothing, old Chiang!
(The Old Man clutches the wall, as though there is an earthquake, shouts to the Magician.)

OLD MAN   Help, Hu-Ming, help! This one here is tossing me into a nightmare again — into China, into the Yangtze, into bloodshed! Awaken me!
(To the Mandarin.)
Come closer...I swear I will not kill you! I heard nothing but a roar, like the collapse of mountains — mountains or entrails!
(To the people.)
Silence, so I can hear! You hang little gold and clay people on Buddha as pledges — and you're appeased! I hang my entrails on him — and I'm not appeased!
I beg you, old sage, dear friend, say it again.
(The Mandarin opens his mouth, but the Old Man rushes toward him and covers it.)
Help, Hu-Ming! Give me a lump of clay, give me a trowel and whitewash and stones so I can plug up his mouth!
(Silence. The Old Man looks dazed at the Mandarin, at his bloodied hands; suddenly a madness overwhelms him and he bursts out in wild, bitter laughter.)
In vain? In vain? In vain?
(The Second Musician rises, takes down the gong, strikes it twice. Curtain.)

ACT III

(Dusk of the same day. The same hall of the Tower. The Old Man is sitting under the panoplies, listening to the canary singing. Now and then he sighs. Suddenly he leaps up and opens the window. The canary stops as the terrible roar of the river is heard.)

OLD MAN   Buddha, Buddha, I think, we're approaching liberation...The world is beginning to be liberated, to thin out, to become transparent. I can make out the river beyond the dark walls,

And beyond the river, the sea; and beyond the sea, old Chiang sailing like a light cloud over Nothingness, unraveling thread by thread and disappearing...

I don't hurt any more, Buddha, may you be well! I'm not afraid, I don't love, I want nothing...Night is falling.

Night is falling, and just as the rider pets his horse to relax it at the end of a journey, so does someone over me — it must be death — caress

My sweating ears, my frothing chest, my bloodied feet.

He frees me from my harness, takes away the bridle, speaks tender words I do not understand — yet I know, this is liberation.

Gratefully I smell its breath in the air.

The villages have drowned, the bells have fallen silent, people no longer raise their hands to cry for help; this, Buddha, must be liberation!

They've folded their hands, sealed their lips; they've understood; they've lain flat on their backs and have surrendered to the Yangtze with trust.

True, true, this is as it should be; our entrails are quiet now, they don't resist, they don't hope, they no longer call on Virtue, that unkissed poison-nosed old maid, to come and defend us.

She, too, lies drowned on her back, surrendered to the current — and there she goes towards the sea...Bless her voyage!

Nor do they even call to Justice or Love any more, to gods or demons...To nothing, to no one!

Poor, wretched man! He's finally realized it: he is alone!

124

Ah, my heart is a sunken city! I lean over, and underneath
the waters I see houses and towers and bones licked clean.
No, no, it's all lies! I see nothing — only a large carcass from
one end of the heart to the other —
A large carcass with glass eyes looking at me — my son!
Be quiet, my heart. Tears are a weakness, laughter is a
weakness, cries are shameful. To whom can we call? I
called to the Ancestors, I fell at their feet, and they gave
their word,
But they've tricked me!
Be quiet, old Chiang, be quiet, old Chiang, don't disgrace
yourself...Why should you lick the foot that kicks you? For
shame! You're not a dog, you're a man; you're not a man,
you're a nobleman;
Hold fast!
(Mei-Ling enters from the large door at left, exhausted, pale.
She looks around.)

MEI-LING   With whom were you talking?

OLD MAN   (Beating his chest.)
With this one!

MEI-LING   You have a fever, your eyes are burning; you're ranting!

OLD MAN   That's how all of you, rotted by the Western World, adjust
yourselves and explain everything. Are your eyes burning?
Then you have a fever! Did you dream the Ancestors were
rising from the earth, armed, and giving orders? It's
nothing, you must have overeaten! Do your ears buzz, do
you hear secret voices in the wind? You're suffering from
blood congestion! Put on some ice packs!
And the soul, what do you do with the soul, Mei-Ling?
(Bends over Mei-Ling, his voice trembling.)
Is it done?

MEI-LING   (Controlling her sobs with difficulty.)
It's done; it's all over.

OLD MAN   Did you hang...

MEI-LING   Yes...yes...a large stone around his neck.

OLD MAN   And...

MEI-LING   Don't ask me!
            (Wails.)
            My brother! My brother!

OLD MAN   *(Tries to caress her hair.)*
            Beloved Mei-Ling!

MEI-LING   *(Drawing back.)*
            Don't touch me!

OLD MAN   You're right!
            (Looks at his hand.)
            Ah, an axe to cut it off! Sometimes I sit and think, Mei-Ling:
            what torture life would be if Death did not come to
            unyoke us.
            Very well, very well, don't frown, Mei-Ling; go on, I'm
            listening: Why did you come? Surely not to stand at my
            aged side this difficult hour.

MEI-LING   No.

OLD MAN   Well? Do you need anything more? Give away everything,
            squander everything, don't ask me!

MEI-LING   The waters are finally nearing the third barrier; the people
            have climbed the tallest trees and are shouting...I've yoked
            all our carts; I've sent boats out; I've saved as many souls
            as I could...

OLD MAN   You've done well!

MEI-LING   They were hungry; I slaughtered a flock of our sheep, and
            they ate.

OLD MAN   You've done well.

MEI-LING   They're cold; shall I order our large ancestral trees to be cut
            down?

OLD MAN   Let them be cut down! The trees long to be cut, to become
            wood; the wood to become fire; the fire to become ashes;
            that is the road,
            Let's follow it, Mei-Ling!

MEI-LING   That's your road: downhill. *I* will fight! I've sent engineers and
            workers, I've ordered them to put strengthening boulders and
            iron bars to reinforce the third barrier; that one will not fall!

126

OLD MAN   (*Sarcastically.*)
Unfortunate little people!
(*As though delerious.*)
And our weathervane, our iron rooster on the rooftop, he too will be drowned.
It's him I pity, him! Why are you staring? You think I don't know what I'm saying? I'm a hundred years old, and I've never spoken with such prudence...
I pity that iron rooster...
Once I talked like you, like prudent little people, and everyone admired me: Nobleman Chiang is prudent! Nobleman Chiang is wise, intelligent, sly! And I was
But a liar, a light-headed sparrow. Now I'm an old eagle and sit on a desolate, hopeless rock and watch the world from on high.
What are you saying? I can't hear; I see only your lips opening and closing...

MEI-LING   I'm not saying anything. I feel you are suffering deeply, and this is the only pleasure I have now.

OLD MAN   (*Trying to laugh.*)
I, suffering? But you should know that I keep getting lighter and lighter. I'm not in pain; don't rejoice yet! I'm jettisoning the ballast, and I'm leaving. I'm jettisoning my son, the Ancestors, hopes, gods — and I'm so much lighter!
I watch my daughter kicking and wanting to leave — and I rejoice...Solitude! Solitude!
I'm jettisoning the world; goodbye little people, I'm leaving!
Eh, Mei-Ling, when I was happy I trembled lest I lose happiness — now I'm relieved.

MEI-LING   There's not enough room here for both of us, old Chiang. The air grows heavy, I'm going.

OLD MAN   The air grows heavy; a daughter hates her old parent.

MEI-LING   Yes.
(*Silence. Suddenly the Old Man bursts into bitter laughter.*)

OLD MAN   Thank you, Buddha, you destroy all the bridges around me; this is what you want. This is what I want, too. Solitude, solitude, wilderness! I admire you, Mei-Ling — you are on

one side, a young girl, a weak, slim reed, and on the other side, the terrible river Yangtze. And you're not shattered, you fight it...
(Silence.)
Mei-Ling, you remind me...
(Stops, moved.)

MEI-LING   What? Your eyes have filled with tears...

OLD MAN   Of the heart of man.
(Abruptly.)
Go! Go cut down the trees, that the people may keep warm...
(Laughs.)
That they may sink warm to the bottom of the river.

MEI-LING   My curse on you, old Chiang!
(Leaves.)

OLD MAN   May you be well, my child.
(To himself.)
The people are crying, "Mercy, mercy!" They're afraid, they're hungry, they're cold...But you, my heart, you scorn mercy now because you have climbed higher and govern the whole circle of futility.

You're serene, because all the agonies of earth have merged inside you and not one is missing. You're without hope and condescension, my heart, because you're proud, and you know.

You know! Why should you shout? To whom shall you speak your pain? You pass noiselessly, slowly over the waters like a mute eagle.

You look at the wheel of the sky turning and grinding the stars; you look at the mind tormented and tied to the wheel, shouting...

You leap, draw circles in the air, trace secrets in the light, signs without order, without meaning...

You play without any purpose, because you're strong; you play by yourself, alone, because you're without hope.

You build towers on the banks of time, you mold gods, sons, and grandsons with water and sand —

You open your eyes, and the creatures come alive; you close your eyes, and they disappear.

You dance, my heart, you dance in the wilderness. You love no
   one, you hate no one, you hope for nothing, you are free!
(Pulls the curtain and gazes at the statue of Buddha that is
bursting with laughter.)
Buddha, Buddha, you are laughing! I know the secret, too,
   I know it, but I cannot laugh.
That's our difference Buddha, no other; and that is why
   you're a god and I'm a worm.
(The slaves arrive carrying a khaki uniform.)
What do you want? What are you holding? Go away!

FIRST SLAVE   You ordered us, Master…It's the uniform of General Chiang…

SECOND SLAVE   Your son's, Master.

OLD MAN   Eh, eh, don't bend your knees; the time has come for all of
   us — masters and slaves — to become one *(Looks at the*
   uniform.) Whose did you say?

FIRST SLAVE   Your son's, Master, Chiang…General Chiang's…

OLD MAN   *(Searching through it.)*
It isn't yellow mist? It isn't twilight clouds? If I blow on it,
   won't it vanish? Eh, eh, come here; don't you, too, try to
   fool me. Is this all that remained? This? Nothing else?
And the flesh that was inside, the bones, the voice, the soul?
   What became of them? You're to bring them to me, do you
   hear? Those are what I want!
(Turns to Buddha.)
We're to blame, Buddha, you're right, we're to blame! If there
   were no parents, Death would die of hunger!
(To the slaves.)
Don't be afraid, I tell you; masters and slaves will all become
   one; the waters are coming to bring justice.

FIRST SLAVE   We kiss your feet, Master, command us. What shall we do
   with these clothes you ordered us to bring you?

OLD MAN   *(Lifting the uniform, looking at it.)*
Is this my son? This? These trousers, this jacket, these bronze
   buttons? Is this my son?
Thirty five years I raised him; he filled out with flesh and
   bones and ideas…And now?

SECOND SLAVE   What shall we do with the clothes, Master, command us.

OLD MAN   Stuff them with air, construct a savage mask of cloth and
              paint, tie everything to a rod, make a scarecrow and nail it
              on the riverbank.
           The river will see it; it will become frightened, they say, and
              turn back.
           (Gasps, tears his shirt open to catch his breath.)
           Ah, I'm smothering!

SLAVES   Master...Master

OLD MAN   *(Recovering.)*
           Ah, is it you, my faithful slaves? You've brought the uniform?
              Why haven't you spoken all this time?
           Fine! Fine! Climb up the wall and hang the uniform beside
              the Ancestors...I cursed you, my son, I cried: "Your
              panoply will not be hung beside the Ancestors' panoplies." I
              disowned you.
           But now, to spite them, stand at their side, my son Chiang.
           Don't growl at me, Ancestors; I've finally reached the edge of
              despair, the cliff of freedom — and I fear no one!
           Don't sharpen your knives again; you can't kill him now, he's
              become immortal, like you. Don't be afraid of them, my
              child, stand beside them.
           *(To the slaves who have climbed the wall to hang up the
           uniform.)*
           A little more to the right...No, no, that's where my own
              armament will hang; more to the right...there!
           (To himself.)
           You have a son, he walks and the earth creaks; and you take
              pride in him and say: "I'm not afraid of death any longer; I
              have a son!" And then you try to touch him,
           And only a uniform of war remains in your hands...
           (The slaves tumble down, terrified.)

FIRST AND
SECOND SLAVES   Master...Master...

OLD MAN   What happened? Did you see something?
           (Points to the Ancestors.)
           Did they tell you anything? Speak!

FIRST SLAVE   There, where we climbed, Master, and were hanging...Ah, ah,
                  I'm still trembling!

130

SECOND SLAVE	I saw...
FIRST SLAVE	*I saw, I*...you were leaning over, you didn't see...
SECOND SLAVE	I did, I swear it, Master...I saw, too; here, touch my hands, they're frozen...
OLD MAN	The whip! *(Searches for the whip.)*
FIRST SLAVE	Don't be angry, Master...Look, all the panoplies have moved and have drawn back!
SECOND SLAVE	As though they don't want to touch your son's clothes...
FIRST SLAVE	As though they were angry; their knives stirred in their belts.
OLD MAN	Go! *(Chases them away with the whip.)* Ancestors, eh, Ancestors, I've done what you wanted, enough now! You gave me a knife, and I returned it as you wanted it — red from tip to haft. Enough now! I, too, have the right to speak; in a few hours I'll descend into the earth; I, too, will become an Ancestor, a great nobleman of earth, like you. Don't be angry. You don't like his company? I like it; he's my son, your grandson, your great-grandson, your great-great-grandson; whether you like it or not, he'll stand beside us, too! *(The large door opens abruptly, Mei-Ling enters and stands at the threshold. She is pale. Silence. The Old Man walks towards her slowly.)*
OLD MAN	Did the third barrier fall?
MEI-LING	Yes.
OLD MAN	And the engineers, the iron rods, the cement, the White Demons? *(Mei-Ling bows her head; the Old Man raises his hands.)* Mei-Ling, my child, man has only one value; haven't you understood that yet? Only one... *(Mei-Ling raises her head as though to question him.)* To watch the Yangtze come, to watch it and not cry out. *(Noise outside. The river waters are heard roaring. The people*

131

fill the Tower courtyards and shout. The slaves run,
frightened, and watch the Old Man, not daring to cross the
threshold.)

OLD MAN   Open the doors!
(The slaves hesitate.)
Open the doors!
(The slaves open the doors, the people rush forward,
terrified.)
Eh, eh, paint your faces, put rouge on your cheeks! What
     faces are these? What mud is this? I don't like it!

PEOPLE   We're lost! Our end has come; we will drown!

OLD MAN   Is this the first time you've thought of death? Is this the first
     time the Black Master-Shepherd has whistled to you in the
     darkness? Get out of my sight, cowards!

PEOPLE   Save us, it's your duty. We're not masters to disdain life; we're
     slaves — we want to eat, to give birth, to fertilize the earth.
It is your duty to save us, old Chiang; save us!

OLD MAN   Don't shout; don't scream; you climb over each other and run
     like rats smelling an earthquake.
(To the Five Whores.)
Why have you brought these white candles? Is this a
     wedding?

PEOPLE   Master, the third dam has fallen!

OLD MAN   I know!
(Beats his chest.)
Now the fourth dam will fall, this one!
(To the Musicians.)
Eh, musicians, let's see what you can do! Play! A great
     Nobleman has reached the foot of our Tower. His Serene
     Highness has condescended to visit us; the great Nobleman
     has arrived with his escort —
Cradles, window shutters, tubs, carcasses, camels and sheep
     and beasts and people — all drowned!
His Serene Highness arrives with his wealthy attendants, layer
     over layer of crocodiles below, layer over layer of crows
     above — and in the middle, the great Nobleman, Yangtze.
Play loudly! Not like that, not like that — joyously!

	(Beating the drum himself.)
	There, like that; as at a wedding, when the bridegroom is coming.
MANDARIN	Hold on to your wits, old Chiang, or they'll leave you. Don't forget you're a nobleman.
OLD MAN	Open the doors! Open both sides! Light the lanterns, all of them! Raise my flags, the green dragons!
PEOPLE	He's gone crazy with grief! Who can save us now? We're lost!
MANDARIN	Make room so I can sit down and listen. Fate has grown savage; each word now has taken on value, it drips with blood and tears; it's my duty to keep it from falling.
	You all depend on me now to be saved or not in the chronicles of China. All of you here will die; I will die, too.
	(Shows his notebook.)
	Only this will remain immortal.
	I see the Magician rising, moving his lips; he wants to speak. Make way, friends, that I may hear and write.
	(Writes. Recites pompously.)
	"Now at this solemn hour, the Magician of that time, Hu-Ming by name, rose, bowed before the Nobleman and said..."
	(To the Mandarin.)
	Speak, Hu-Ming, I'm writing.
MAGICIAN	*(Bowing before the Old Man.)*
	Shall I begin? Shall I bring Buddha down again, to relieve your heart, my Nobleman?
	You'll see, everything's but mist and clouds. The strong wind, the Spirit, will blow, and everything will scatter...
	And your bloodied hands, old Chiang, will turn white, as white as the moon.
	(Softer.)
	Old Chiang, there is no other salvation.
OLD MAN	I know.
MAGICIAN	Shall I begin?
OLD MAN	Wait...wait...My heart still has room, it can contain everything shamelessly. Don't be in such a hurry...

(*To the women who are holding the white candles.*)
Why are you carrying these white candles?

MANDARIN (*Approaches the Old Man, trembling.*)
It's an old custom, my nobleman, to save the people...

OLD MAN You don't answer? Why do we need white candles?
(*To the Mandarin.*)
You, be quiet!

WOMEN (*Falling at Mei-Ling's feet.*)
Oh, Mei-Ling, young noble lady...

MEI-LING Why are you kissing my feet? Get up!

WOMEN Pity us, noble lady, save us!

MEI-LING I? I?

WOMEN Only you can save us, my lady...

MEI-LING Oh, if only I could save you! If only my soul might not
vanish but be built as a foundation in the mud...a
foundation for China...
(*To the women.*)
Why don't you speak? How can I save you? Why are you
crying?
(*To the Mandarin.*)
Old scribe, I caught sight of you talking with the women;
what do they want?

MANDARIN It's an old custom, my lady, to save the people...to tame the
river...

WOMEN Today, my lady, as you crossed the river, we saw...
The Old River's back was swelling, swelling like a tiger that
sees his female...
It's you it wants, my lady, it's you it's looking for, it's
aroused now and is descending to drown us...

MANDARIN An old custom, my lady, to save the people...to tame the
river...
What are you thinking of, my lady?

MEI-LING Nothing...nothing...
(*Suddenly lets out a harrowing cry.*)
My brother, I'm coming!

MANDARIN	I swear I heard the River murmuring and wailing like a human..."The noble lady, the noble lady..." it murmured and sighed, "the noble young lady..."
OLD MAN	*(Who has been listening. Now he rushes savagely, stands in front of Mei-Ling and spreads out his arms.)* No, no, enough! My son died in vain, only she is left me... Enough!
MEI-LING	Let me be, father...let me be...and let me vanish, for my only joy now is on that other shore.
OLD MAN	No, no, I won't let you! Enough now!
WOMEN	Mei-Ling, the great moment comes once in a lifetime, only once – to become or not to become immortal. The entire soul hangs, Mei-Ling, on the movement of a hand, on the rise and fall of an eyebrow, on one small word... Move your hand, Mei-Ling, let your eyebrows rise and fall, say "yes" Mei-Ling...
OLD MAN	No, no, I will not let her go – I have no one else! Ah, I thought my heart had become stone, that when struck, it shot sparks – but it's a sick, complaining monkey that weeps...No, no, I will not let her go!
MANDARIN	Master, do not trample the holy customs of the Ancestors. Rivers are great male beasts, Master...When they get angry, they want a woman to calm them...It's an old custom – the noble lady of the land is dressed and adorned like a bride, and then thrown into the river. The river's a man, you see, and he wants to embrace; he embraces and at once shrivels up, his strength softens, he looks at the world and pities it – he understands now the meaning of gentleness, of child, of the embrace – and he turns back. Listen, Master... *(Opens the book, searches, reads.)* "During the glorious kingdom of the Mings when the king was..."
OLD MAN	*(Grabs the book and tramples on it with fury.)* Shut your mouth!
MANDARIN	*(Jumping back in terror.)*

The Ancestors...the Ancestors are in there...Books are sacred, like cemeteries.

OLD MAN   *(Sarcastically.)*
The Ancestors! I'm not afraid of them any more; I'm free! He was right, this one!
(Points to Chiang's uniform.)
My son, Chiang!
I'm free of Ancestors, I'm free of graves!
(Smiles bitterly.)
Too late...too late...at this moment I'm entering the graveyard...

PEOPLE   We're lost! What blasphemies are these, Master? You're shaking the foundations of the world.

OLD MAN   Enough, I say! So I'm shaking the foundations of the world? Brainless cowards, but haven't you understood it yet? The foundations of the world are smoke and air!
Go back! I gave up my son for nothing! For nothing!
(Points to the panoplies.)
They fooled me! Good for them!
(To the Magician.)
I wish I knew, Hu-Ming, where all that lost pain of man goes and settles. Somewhere on the earth — not in the sky, nor in Hades — somewhere on the earth, our Mother, there must be the large reservoirs where the tears of men are gathered — and one day these will overflow.
This must be the terrible Yangtze of man. Yes, yes, it is! And then, joy to the living! The gods will sit on their stools, gods and men will open their large ledgers, they'll come to an accounting — this is what we gave, men will say, so many barrels of tears, so many cisterns of sweat, so many rivers of blood.
And what was our share? A poor uncultivated strip of field, all thorns and stones, a dark, ill-fated brain, a woman full of teeth and nails and cries — the final bill will be issued and the gods will pay.
All then, Hu-Ming, all will be paid, all of it!
(To the People.)
Why are you crowding around me? Go! I said I will not give her. Let the bridegroom himself come and take her.

PEOPLE   It will be on your conscience.

OLD MAN:	Let it be on my conscience; I will not give her!
MANDARIN	Say yes, Old Chiang, say yes, give her willingly, otherwise the sacrifice won't succeed.
PEOPLE	*(They surround the Old Man threateningly as the circle becomes narrower.)* Say yes, Old Man, to save us!
OLD MAN	*(Trying to break the circle smothering him.)* Do you want to choke me? Go away!
PEOPLE	Say yes...
OLD MAN	No!
MANDARIN	Think of your grandson!
OLD MAN	Don't try to frighten me, you penpusher! My grandson is far, far away, safe; I no longer fear anything! He will fill my fields with men again. No, the Dynasty of Chiang will not vanish! So long as my grandson lives, I am immortal. Yes, yes, I played the Yangtze's game, I've fooled it! *(Old Koag suddenly appears at the large door, wet, muddied, holding the grandson in his arms. The Old Man starts, cuts through the crowd, stands before Koag and shouts.)* No! No!
OLD KOAG	Master...
OLD MAN	No, no, it's not you!
OLD KOAG	Master, forgive me...
OLD MAN	No, no, I say! My eyes are on fire, my ears are buzzing... Mei-Ling, help! I see ghosts, I hear ghosts, help! Who is this before me?
MEI-LING	Koag, old Koag, our faithful slave.
OLD MAN	What is he holding in his arms? The truth! Speak the truth; don't pity me.
MEI-LING	Your grandson, father.
OLD MAN	Who?
OLD KOAG.	The river flooded the valley, Master...I rushed with the

oxcart, the oxen were drowned, the water rose to my neck;
I held your grandson over my head...
I took another road; I've been struggling since dawn —
I shouted, I pleaded, I fought — I could not get through,
forgive me.

PEOPLE   Master, you've played your game now with the Yangtze...

OLD MAN   May it be cursed! If only it had a body, if only it were a
man! But it's all slime and water and can't be grasped...
Oh, if I, old Chiang, were a river, too, I'd rush upon it and
fight it!
(As though seeing Koag for the first time.)
Koag, you here? You've returned?

OLD KOAG   Master, forgive me...

OLD MAN   A curse on hope! Wretched man forgets himself for a moment
and says: "Perhaps there's a door open...perhaps. Very
small, like the footstep of a baby..."
And he runs to slip through, to save himself — and becomes
degraded.
I've lost the game; I, too, raise my hands, Mei-Ling; I
surrender.
I cross my oars, I cross my hands, I cross my brain, I give
myself up to the torrent. I shout: "Eh, torrent, wherever
you're going, I too have been going. I'm glad you've come;
I leap and mount you bareback! Let's be off!"
Nothing bothers me now; I've reached the summit of pain;
from there on liberation begins!
(To his grandson.)
Come here, you!
(Grabs him in his arms, caresses him.)
Quiet, quiet, my child, we've lost the game...
Mei-Ling, good luck to you, go.
*(The Women run to Mei-Ling, throw a white veil over her
and place a wreath of flowers on her head. The white candles
lead the procession. The Old Man turns to Mei-Ling and
speaks calmly.)*
Mei-Ling, are you leaving?

MEI-LING   I'm leaving, father.

OLD MAN   In vain...all in vain...

138

MEI-LING   I know. Does it matter, father?

OLD MAN   No, it doesn't matter; go. If you see anyone down there, tell
          him I'm coming.

MEI-LING   *(Smiling.)*
           I'll see worms.

OLD MAN   Tell them I'm coming.
          *(The Women light the white candles. Mei-Ling calmly falls on
          her knees and kisses the ground.)*

MEI-LING   Sun, rain, plow, dung, beloved grass, O China, farewell.
           (Falls at the Old Man's feet.)
           Father, forgive me; until this morning I was still very young,
              very cruel, deaf, blind, armed with hopes...But now, at
              last, I understand.
           Father, place your bloodied hands on my head; give me your
              blessing; I'm leaving.

OLD MAN   *(Places his hands on Mei-Ling's head.)*
          My blessings on you, Mei-Ling.
          This, Buddha, is the most humiliating torture: to see your
             loved one leaving forever, forever, forever — and not feel
             sad.
          What is the soul, then? Mud? But even mud remembers your
             footprint when you step on it.
          (To Mei-Ling.)
          Farewell! Farewell! If I lived on, I'd build you a temple,
             Mei-Ling, small and charming, like your body, a temple on
             the banks of the Yangtze where you may be worshipped.
          And over the doorway I'd insert a bronze plaque, and on it I'd
             engrave with embellished and sacred letters:
          "Mei-Ling, nobleman Chiang's beautiful, young, virgin
             daughter, Mei-Ling, married the nobleman Yangtze to save
             her country. In vain! In vain! In vain! O passerby, toss a
             white wildflower on the river waters and cry three times:
             'In vain! In vain! In vain!'"

MEI-LING   *(Smiling bitterly.)*
           Yes, father.

OLD MAN   But I'm not going to live, I won't build a temple, I won't
          engrave a bronze plaque — does it matter, Mei-Ling?

139

MEI-LING   It doesn't matter, father. Farewell.

OLD MAN   Wait, don't leave yet, my child; do me this last favor: give me
            your blessing.

MEI-LING   I?

OLD MAN   Give me your blessing, my child.

MEI-LING   Beloved father, I remember the hawk I dreamt about, that
            ate all your flesh, strip by strip...
            I cannot speak any more, farewell.
            (To the Women.)
            Let us go.
            *(The Women take Mei-Ling, pass the threshold at right,
            descend the steps singing wedding songs softly. The Old Man
            runs to the window, tightens his arms around his grandchild
            and shouts.)*

OLD MAN   My child!
            (To Buddha.)
            Here I am, Buddha, just as you wanted me: they've plucked
                my two great wings, my son Chiang and my daughter,
                Mei-Ling — only the worm remains.
            Break, O my small heart; aren't you ashamed to endure?
                Break at last, to show your nobility.
            O Buddha, you kill all, without being bloodthirsty; you
                show compassion to everything, without being
                compassionate. Your laughter is a cataract made of all
                mankind's tears; and your own tears Buddha, are the pure,
                refined, and distilled quintessence of all the people's
                laughter.
            (To his grandson.)
            This is Buddha, your plaything, my child; do not be afraid.

PEOPLE   *(With agony.)*
            Has the river grown calm? It's still roaring...Help us!

MANDARIN   Don't be in such a hurry. God is in no hurry, and that's why
            he is God...When he's had enough, he'll remember the
            people and perform his miracle.

OLD MAN   Quiet; I can't bear you any longer! What will grow calm? The
            river? The river? My curses on virtue, sacrifice, nobility! I
            am caught, entangled in my own virtues, and that's why I

140

	can never escape.
	The free man has no friend; not even death.
MAGICIAN	Old Chiang, my nobleman...
MANDARIN	He doesn't hear; he's floating on deep waters...speak louder to him.
MAGICIAN	Old Chiang!
OLD MAN	Ah! Is it you, Madam Imagination, you versatile whore? Where were you when I lost my way? We haven't met for years and years...
MAGICIAN	Years, my Nobleman?
OLD MAN	You see, Hu-Ming, each drop of time became heavy — like a corpse with a rock hung around its neck and tossed into the waves.
	Where are you, Hu-Ming? Give me your hand.
	Hu-Ming, resourceful thinker, forgive me, I take back my harsh words; the free man has *one* friend: you.
MAGICIAN	My Nobleman, the waters have risen up to here
	(Indicates his neck.)
	The mouth will remain free for a little while. It still has one cry, one free cry inside it. Don't let it vanish, my Nobleman, don't let it vanish in the grave.
OLD MAN	The cry of freedom must not vanish, Hu-Ming, my beloved, it must not vanish into the grave; you are right.
	And when the whole world is drowned, that cry will still fly over the waters and shout.
MAGICIAN	Onward then, let's not waste time. I rally my brave co-workers — the wings, the yellow mask, the twelve signs of the zodiac, the multi-colored words, the difficult rhymes, the gaudy metaphors, the eyes, the ears, the fiery wind, the Dance, and Music, and the Word — the father, the mother, and the son!
	(To the Second Musician.)
	Beat the drum; I'm ordering a mobilization!
OLD MAN	My blessings on you, Hu-Ming. Get a good start, lift man above man. But quickly, for I feel the water under

my chin.

MANDARIN   *(To the Magician.)*
Aren't you ashamed! Have you no heart? Don't you see the people weeping? We're lost! We're lost, and you, you cheap actor, are you still playing?

MAGICIAN   Where did we stop, my Nobleman? Do you remember?

OLD MAN   Don't ask; at the edge of the precipice — give us another shove, push us over.

MAGICIAN   Farewell, people, farewell old Chiang. If I said anything that sets heavy on your heart, forgive me; if I said anything to lighten your heart, if I did you some good, forgive me. I bid you farewell, farewell, because I don't know if I'll come out of this performance alive...
I'm afraid for you, too, old Chiang.

OLD MAN   Don't be afraid for me; my heart is a closed-in garden of rocks, no tree, no water, no grass, just stone.
And the garden is filled with birds: with crows. Speak fearlessly.
(The Magician makes the circle, pins down the twelve signs of the zodiac, says an exorcism.)

MAGICIAN   Are you ready, old Chiang?

OLD MAN   I'm ready.

MAGICIAN   Can you endure one more word, the last I have to tell you?

OLD MAN   Go on, I tell you, I can.

MAGICIAN   The One divided, old Chiang, and we are to blame; the One divided and became Life and Death.
Before we were born, He was One; as soon as we die, He will become One again; it's we who get in the middle and thwart Him.
Life is an eclipse of God; let's draw back, old Chiang, that His entire face may shine.

OLD MAN   Let's step back, Hu-Ming, that His entire face may shine.
Buddha, stretch out your hand, bless these creatures who moan at your feet — stretch out your hand and drown them.

Help man, Lord, to leap across the terrible threshold, without
mind or memory, without fire, without water and earth
and wind — free at last!

MAGICIAN   O Mind, who are all-powerful, help me!
*(Puts on the yellow mask and immediately the set changes; we
return to the vision.)*

PEOPLE   What is that sound, that fluttering of wings, those flashes of
sparks on the stones? Clouds have gathered in the sky.
Don't shout! It's the disciples of Buddha — some mounted on
gigantic wings, some on the backs of lions, some riding on
white clouds...
Some come from the sky, others rip through the earth and
ascend; some have taken to the river, sit cross-legged on
water-lilies and sail with the tide...
One sings, another falls silent; one thinks, another cries.
Each with his own given aptitude rejoices in liberation.

YOUNG MAN   And that woman, who is that woman, without hair,
without breasts, dressed in a saffron robe, holding a long
fan of peacock feathers and fanning Buddha...
The elephants have slowly turned their round, calm eyes
toward Buddha and their brows glow, as though it were
dawning;
And the little beasts, the weasels, the foxes, the squirrels, the
ferrets, rise on their hind legs, as though the moon had
suddenly appeared.
And with erect tails, satiated, without a care, they begin to
dance around Buddha.
Oh, the earth has filled with disciples in saffron robes. One
goes in front, fat and serene, riding a white-browed cow,
and advances, well-nourished, toward nonexistence.
And beside him a ferocious ascetic strides over the earth,
exhausted with holiness and hunger.
I see a huge-bodied disciple, bursting with strength and rage,
approaching, stomping like a gorilla. He is speaking with
invisible enemies, explaining the teachings as he raises his
fist and beats the air.
And behind him another disciple, bathed, painted, smiling,
with a heavy gold earring, with a valuable fan of white
ostrich feathers, follows the procession slowly, proudly.

143

Mogalana — look at him, brothers! — has rushed among the
disciples, embracing, kissing, greeting the comrades of the
struggle, and their bronze begging-bowls clang joyously,
like war shields;

And Saripoutta is standing quietly, silently, sunk in ecstasy,
rejoicing in nothing.

The dancing swells, the faces of the disciples glow, their songs
have caught fire! The smiling, newly-bathed disciple speaks
first, slowly, calmly, as though singing a lullaby to an
infant child, as though exorcising

The invisible spirits of virtue and of evil.

FIRST DISCIPLE   We waken, descend to the river, we wash, clean and polish
our swords — our bodies.

We ascend with the sun and go, glittering, serenely and
without hope, toward the city.

We stand erect beside the low doors of the people, and for
many hours wait for a crumb, with patience and
acquiescence.

And when the holy begging ends, we return, again with the
sun, and sink like gold worms in the forest. We gather
leaves, and then sit cross-legged with head erect, as the
circumference of our faces shines from unsleeping
contemplation.

Motionless and smiling, we release the power of our mercy to
go forward, to flood the North; to go back, to flood the
South; then to the right to reach the East, and then to the
left to reach the West.

And then to rush to the sky's zenith to abolish the good
powers, the gods; and to descend below, deep into Tartarus
to abolish the evil powers, the demons.

Almighty is our power; as quiet as sleep, as sweet as death;
it floods the world and tames the five great ghosts — wind,
earth, fire, water and the spirit.

PEOPLE   A slender, young disciple gets up to dance, but changes his
mind, then throws himself down and weeps.

The bountiful grace of Buddha must have fallen upon him and
he cannot bear it.

Ah, the savage disciple has taken the lead in the dance, his
brain has caught fire and he begins singing.

144

SECOND DISCIPLE   Buddha's word is a conflagration! We did not come to make
                   the homes of men secure. We did not come to plant, to
                   marry people or to bless phalluses and wombs.
                   We are quiet, simple, and wait with patience — but when the
                   thunderbolt is deserved, then even more unwaveringly than
                   the god Indra, we hurl it on earth!
                   Fire is our bread and wine, fire is our home and our wife. Fire
                   is our plow, and we came to plow, to open and cleanse the
                   earth, and to plant burning coals,
                   Our holy seed.

PEOPLE   A pale disciple is blushing, he can't restrain himself and begins
                   a song, singing like a woman in love;
                   His almond-shaped, downy eyes sparkle and play.

THIRD DISCIPLE   Lord, Lord, when I am far away from you and hear your
                   voice proclaiming liberation,
                   Then my breast melts, Lord, my knees tremble and I am lost.
                   A deep precipice opens between every other word you
                   speak, Lord, a deep precipice, and I fall into it.
                   But when I approach and see you, Lord, my heart grows
                   calm, my knees grow strong, and I walk firmly from one
                   word to the other — as when we jump from rock to rock
                   over the water in crossing a stream.
                   And when I sit at your feet and touch you, Lord, everything
                   disappears...There are no rocks, there are no waters, there
                   is no onward march; I was a lighted candle and I've melted
                   away.

PEOPLE   Oh, the hungry, flesh-eaten ascetic has taken up the song.
                   The trees, the waters and the beasts have fallen silent to
                   hear him.

FOURTH DISCIPLE   I sit, quietly blissful, my hands empty, my entrails empty, my
                   heart empty...I love no one, I hate no one, I want nothing.
                   I say: I am not perfect, I will be reborn; and I feel no
                   sadness. I say: I am perfect, I will not be reborn; and I feel
                   no joy.
                   I've escaped from my father and mother, I've deserted my
                   wife and my children, I have thrown off my burdens. I've
                   escaped from gods and demons, I've escaped from hope,
                   and my bones whistle and sing like the reeds of a
                   dilapidated hut.

145

I've escaped from the flesh and the spirit; I walk airily over
   heads, like a cloud, and the people in the fields rejoice and
   say: "It will rain, the earth will become cool again, the
   seedlings will ripen."
And I pass over them without rain, without coolness, without
   a wind. I am
A small, small, parched thought belonging to Buddha.

MOUDITA　　*(To her husband, the young man.)*
Why are you staring at me? I'm not a bitch, I'm not a
   dilapidated hut, I'm not a ghost; I'm not your wife.
I am a reed on the riverbank of Buddha.

YOUNG MAN　　A curse on God who leads man to such perfection!
Come back beloved Moudita, come back again to man's warm
   body and save yourself.

MOUDITA　　I am a reed on the riverbank of Buddha; ah, when will I
   become the sound of a flute, to fade away?

PEOPLE　　I'm afraid, brother. Buddha doesn't look, he doesn't speak or
   move...He sits cross-legged underneath the dry Tree and
   his head, his hands, his feet glitter.
The head of Buddha has grown large, it has flared up like the
   sun, whitened like fiery iron; no one can go near him.
Mogalana has bared his right shoulder, he has taken a step
   forward with much pain, he has taken another, but he's
   panting, he can't go on; the earth shook in seven different
   ways beneath his feet;
And Mogalana has turned back and clutches Saripoutta so as
   not to fall.

YOUNG MAN　　Buddha, I gaze upon you and my skull empties, my brain
   spills out, my spine drips over the abyss,
Ah, in vain did I sink into the five pits of my body like a pig,
   to escape from you.

BLOSSOMING　　Lord, pity the men!
CHERRY TREE　　Cast all your rage mercilessly upon me, the woman, O
   Savior!
The man, Lord, is always ready for salvation, but I won't let
   him. The man sits at the river's edge, crosses his legs,
   crosses his heart and his mind, and swears:

146

"I will not eat, I will not drink, I will not sleep with woman;
I seek salvation."
But Lord, I pass by, my eye catches sight of him and I yearn
for his savagery, his strength and his ugliness; all at once a
fire leaps between my two breasts and I say: "I want to
sleep with him! I want to sleep with him!"
My breasts weigh me down Lord, they are heavy, full of
milk, I can't walk! I hurt; I want a son to clutch my
nipples, to drink all of me.
I wander through the mountains, walk through the cities,
enter temples, sit at windows – and call to men.
It's not I who call, Lord; it's my mother inside me who calls,
that hairy ancestor, an inconsolable female beast calls from
inside me – the entire Earth.
Put out this fire in my entrails, Lord, and save the world.
The abyss shrank, became body, became voice, bathed,
painted and adorned itself, sprouted breasts, became a
woman. Ah, I waste my strength in merging with the abyss.
The mind of Buddha turns, turns, ascends, descends, eats up
the earth.
His chins move and grind; the blood and brains of all men
flow from his lips.
Don't look to the right, don't look to the left, no one can
escape. Let's not resist, let's proceed with a quiet, firm
tread, freely toward that mouth.
I want to leave! I want to leave! I left my son in his cradle;
who will suckle him? I left my husband at the plow; who
will bring him food?
Buddha will suckle him, don't worry, my sister; and Buddha
will feed your husband with earth.
Buddha, Buddha, mercy! My heart is a piece of meat and
fat, Lord, and it believes in bread, in the child and in the
flesh; don't kill me!
Don't shout at it; it doesn't hear, it doesn't speak, it doesn't
move; don't degrade yourself. The world is a river, a river
that spills over
Into the pit of your eye.
I can see a dark well in the center of the earth and we all run
hurriedly, fighting, laughing, crying, and we all fall into
the well
With bloodied cotton wadding in our mouths.

This is not a well, brothers; this is the third, the secret eye of Buddha, that lies unmoving between his eyebrows and swallows us.

MANDARIN   Don't be afraid my children. I'll rise and defend you. I'll call the three great gods, I'll cast exorcisms in the wind; I'll force the invisible powers to take on flesh and descend from the air;

Brahma, Siva, Vishnu, help me!

The air flashed, it moved! Brahma, that crimson lion, treads on the nine levels of the sky, step by step, and descends.

As blue-green as poison, Siva wraps a snake seven-fold around his loins and descends; and Vishnu, cross-legged upon a green leaf, serenely balancing his two arms to the right and left, slowly flutters to the ground.

Behind him numberless battalions descend from the nine skies …The spirits sit cross-legged on multi-colored carpets where their kingdoms glow embroidered

With red, yellow, and green air.

Oh! Oh! Like the shed leaves of autumn the gods fall to the earth.

And Mogalana has bared his right shoulder with reverence, has taken two strides and stands like a nobleman of the earth, welcoming them.

MOGALANA   I bow and greet the head of the world, the wind of life, the onrush of breath, Brahma.

I sit cross-legged in the silence of night, encircled by the dark powers; and Earth, that painted and primped whore, begins to dance in my mind;

And you rise, Brahma, you fix your eyes upon her — this Earth to you seems like a woman, the sea stretches across your temples like a wide bed, and all at once you leap from my head like sperm, and say:

"I want to fill her womb with children!"

And I let you escape from my mind, to merge, to spill into the imagination that generations may multiply, that flesh may be molded, that spirits may struggle, that elements may suffer and pass through every exploit, and I meditate:

This earth is a precious, multi-colored, nonexistent essence, and the husband of this essence, Brahma, is precious,

148

multi-colored and nonexistent; let's rejoice, serene and unruffled, in the merging of this holy couple.

I bow and worship to your grace. May you be welcome, O Brahma, O bridegroom. Approach with reverence and curl up like a gold insect in Buddha's palm.

PEOPLE Oh, oh, Brahma extends his begging-bowl to Buddha in supplication.

BRAHMA Lord, Lord, you built me tall, strong and righteous; you gave me hands, feet, a heart, a head. I was hungry, and you nurtured me with hymns. I was thirsty, and you gave me your palms filled with the tears of men, and I drank and was intoxicated.

You said: "Just as salt seasons the whole sea and no one can separate the two, so does Brahma invisibly penetrate the Universe." — I believed you, and rushed to give taste and savor to the Universe.

Lord, I am tired, pity me! Open your mouth and give me the signal for liberation. I'm tired now of standing upright; all this turbulence of the elements is but a meaningless absurdity, a heavy illness; life is a futile intoxication.

We suffer, we shout, we contaminate the air with our breathing, we contaminate the waters with our tears, we infect death with our bodies.

Lord, give me the supremest health, give me the clearest, most sober meditation — complete obliteration. Think secretly in the pit of your mind: "Brahma does not exist!" and I will disappear. Look upon me with mercy Lord, that I may vanish.

PEOPLE Buddha reaches out his hand, places a small ball of earth between Brahma's lips, and Brahma falls silent.

Siva rolls down before him like a wheel all arms and legs...Look at him, look: he stops now and begins to tremble.

MOGALANA I welcome Siva, the savage and gallant youth of the Unreal!

You shout: "Shatter, earth, that I may pass. Open, sky, that I may enter. Break, heart, that I may nestle.

I don't want them, I hate the creations of Brahma! Who said that flesh or the brain could contain me?

149

Mogalana, step back, I am Siva, I am the Great Fire, the
beginning and the end. Shatter into pieces, Mogalana, that
I may pass!"
You shout and shout, and I hold you in my palm, Siva, I
smile and say: "A small poisoned scorpion is Siva; let him
stand away in fear from Buddha's burning coals."

PEOPLE   Quiet, brothers; Siva extends his begging-bowl to Buddha in
supplication.

SIVA   Lord, I cannot make the people vanish. They're like ants
creeping out of the earth; I uproot a son —
And ten sons and daughters sprout in his place.
I ride on a black horse and unite the ends of the earth; I hang
clusters of slaughtered souls on my saddle like partridges;
doors shut, streets become deserted, people whirl, turn pale
and fall —
And suddenly, behind me, as I pass, under the trees, inside
caves, amidst ruins, I hear men and women embracing,
and flocks of little children chasing me...Wherever I pass
the earth cracks; I swallow villages, I dance on skulls and
shout: "The seed of man has been liquidated, it's been
wiped out, the earth has been disburdened!" But suddenly
from the ruins a girl fourteen years old appears, and from
the mountain top a chubby shepherd boy descends — and
they unite laughing and shrieking on the stones.
And then, in their happiness, they build a firm hearth, they
gather wood, light a fire, pound branches into the earth,
build a hut, eat, kiss, sleep, gather strength, waken.
The man goes to work, plows, sows, pens his sheep, milks
them, whistles at his dogs, goes hunting;
And the woman draws water from the well, sets the caldron
over the fire, prepares the food, sits at the threshold,
opens her breasts and suckles her son.
Ah Lord, man and woman kiss with such lavish sweetness
that life cannot be wiped out. Like wheat, a dead man is
thrust into the ground, but in nine months' time he sprouts
and rises, a wheat stalk armed with seeds, a grandson from
the soil.
I'm tired of fighting men; I raise my hands and surrender;
help me to die, Buddha.

PEOPLE　　Buddha stretches out his hand, places a small lump of earth between Siva's lips and silences him.

MOGALANA　Quiet, brothers. The great god Vishnu is in a hurry to approach and speak of his pain, too.
Vishnu, balanced reason, firm step among two frenzied dancers, Brahma and Siva,
Welcome!
You stand for a moment above chaos, unafraid, O skillful Tightrope Walker, and smiling gallantly, dance to the right, dance to the left, and greet everyone politely
Before you fall into chaos.
You hold a scale between your eyebrows, you weigh and mingle visible and invisible powers, tiptoeing on the high, taut rope, and you reflect:
"The world is a delicate game of scales. I tremble over the abyss, I grow dizzy; fearful visions of gods, men, beasts and ideas rise in my head. I can't endure it any longer! Ah, when will I finally fall headlong and find relief!"
Great Vishnu, my weary athlete, approach with trust, don't tremble; smile, bid the empty air farewell for the last time, and rest, O great martyr,
Within the azure certainty of Buddha.

PEOPLE　　Great, sacred moment! Vishnu, the mightiest god of all, extends his begging-bowl to Buddha in supplication.

VISHNU　　Lord, Lord, you placed me in a cool darkness where I sit cross-legged; and my eyes shine like a well-fed lion's, rested, calm, without cunning. I cock my ears and hear the footsteps of the faithful gliding over the flagstones lightly, fearful
Of waking me from my holy sleep.
My fists overflow with fruits, flowers and warm offerings, with spices and honey...
A maiden places a white rose in my open palm and secretly confesses: "The sun has darkened me, my Lord; make me white that I may be pleasing."
And a poor field-worker unfolds his apron, heaps my fist with wheat and prays: "Father, rise, look out of your temple door — our fields are thirsty, the soil has hardened and holds the seed in idleness. Rain, Lord, that we may not die

151

of hunger."

And a mother behind him rushes out and places her dead boy
on my knees. She screams, fixes her eyes upon me and
commands: "Resurrect him!"

And I hold the terrible burden in my arms and weep secretly,
sensing God's incurable misery.

Buddha, Buddha, I walk trembling on a taut hair stretched
over two precipices, and I hold two red apples to balance
myself — death in my right hand and life in my left.

I know, Lord, that a balanced mind is the greatest virtue and
nobility of god and of man; I know, but I can endure no
more. I'm tired, Lord, and I tremble over the abyss; pity me!

I can't keep my balance; I want to fall. Raise your hand,
Buddha, and order the tightrope walking to end.

PEOPLE   Buddha stretches out his hand, places a small lump of earth
between Vishnu's lips and silences him.

The Gods have been reduced to phantoms of the mind, to
great ideas, to gaudy metaphors, and all of them carry
bowls and beg for alms.

MOGALANA   The gods approached Buddha, turned into myths and fainted
in the air.

As when we throw three water-lilies into the funnel of a great
river to amuse ourselves, and they dance, shine, twist and
turn for a moment like three heads and suddenly are
swallowed up by the whirlpool,

So has Buddha swallowed the three great gods.

Don't shout, don't cry, don't be glad; Buddha but turned the
wheel of earth a little faster and the Universe vanished.

MANDARIN   Oh Mind, last-born god, clear, faultless eye! The elements
have rebelled again, they've broken their chains, they've
leaped from chaos and torn down the boundaries of reason.

They're drunk, Lord; all certainties have gone astray, all
numbers have adorned themselves with gaudy feathers, like
parrots.

I shout, I command, but my voice boomerangs in chaos and
strikes me like a stone. I hold the great keys of reason in
my hands, and I lock, unlock and dislocate but air.

Come down, all-powerful Mind, and bring order to Chaos!

PEOPLE   The water-brained God of Wisdom is coming, he's stooping

152

down and rummaging through the earth, smelling and
ransacking the graveyards.

He stops confused and looks around him; he's trapped, he
wants to leave, but he cannot.

MOGALANA   Welcome, welcome newborn beast of human arrogance! Your
legs buckle under, you are knock-kneed, you stagger and
stumble, you can't lift your pumpkin head, as heavy as an
elephant's.

Your loins, O wretched God of Wisdom, are drained; your
phallus has shrivelled and hangs like a withered apple; your
heart is a bag of questions: "Whence? And where? And
why?"

Don't tremble; yes, yes, it's I, do you remember? It's
Mogalana.

One day I entered your kingdom to converse with you; you
went ahead proudly and showed me your Palace —

"These are my gardens, my peacocks, my fountains; these
are my soft beds, my wives, my sons, my slaves...And
these all round about are my overflowing cellars..."

And as you crowed, O royal rooster, I thought: "This god
lives too brazenly." And as I was thinking this, O God of
Wisdom, I summoned up an earthquake and your Palace
toppled.

But now I see you've taken courage again and have come to
this holy gathering. What do you want?

GOD OF WISDOM   To leave! To leave!

MOGALANA   Have you lost your wits?

GOD OF WISDOM   Yes, I've lost my wits. What kind of world is this? What
rebellion! The laws have taken wing, they've gone! I pick
up a pebble to measure it but I can't take its measurement,
for as I touch it, it lengthens, widens, thins out and at
times

Becomes a cloud, at times a turkey puffed up like a
nobleman, and at other times a ship with full sails cruising
on the ground.

I want to leave, to leave! I've lugged my tools here in vain —
the measure, the compass, the level, the scale, my
notebooks...Who calls me?

153

MANDARIN	I called you, Lord; I, your faithful servant, who holds *The Chronicles of Man*.
	Lord, Lord, save the world! Look, Buddha, the proud rebel of Thought, sits under the Tree quietly, motionless, and winds the world around the reel of his power.
	Raise your omnipotent voice, Lord, and exorcise him! Lord, don't you hold the bow of truth eternally taut? Shoot him with your deadly arrow!
GOD OF WISDOM	Don't shout, let me go! My arrows must find flesh in order to kill; otherwise they are useless.
	How can I fight the air? How can I wound dreams?
MANDARIN	If you cannot wound dreams, we are lost, Lord!
MOGALANA	Ah, the wingless, four-cornered brain couldn't find firm ground here on which to walk; it has ascended to the upper level and grows dizzy!
	You see, Buddha is not flesh to be eaten; he's not stone to be built; Buddha is a compassionate precipice beyond the brain, beyond your scales and your levels, miserly Hoarder of Wisdom!
	O bubble, you've risen very high, you've reached the feet of Buddha where the air is thin and rare — and you will burst!
	Aha! You've burst, you've deflated, you've become lighter! Your gigantic head was but a wind-bag!
PEOPLE	Gone, scattered are the notebooks, the scales, the levels of the God of Wisdom. They've become butterflies and flutter around Buddha's shoulders.
	They've become cool, multi-colored fans to refresh him.
	Quiet; two strangers have appeared dressed in short white tunics with wild olive wreaths crowning their curly hair. Handsome, sun-burned, happy.
	They seem to be gods of a naive, newly-born people. Be quiet, old Mandarin, don't cry, so we may hear what they're saying.
FIRST GREEK	Beloved fellow-traveller, I believe we've reached the goal of our great journey. Motionless and pellucid in our minds now shine the mountains, the waters, the countless villages, all the barbaric riches our insatiable eyes have accepted and stored.

On this, our spiritual Asiatic expedition.
I never knew the world was so large, that one could travel
for years outside the bright boundaries of Greece, could
pass plains and mountains and waters as the foundations
of the sky opened unceasingly and the earth seemed to have
no end.

SECOND GREEK   And I never knew, beloved comrade, that beauty has so many
faces, that so many roads lead to the eternal good, and
that people with barbaric speech exist who love, hurt and
feel the way we Greeks do;
And that they, too, shape thoughts and statues with wood,
stone and the mind.
When I return to Greece, with the power of Hermes the
Traveller, and re-enter my sunlit workshop with its many
unfinished statues of gods,
I shall paint the lips of Athena crimson, I shall hang thick
curls on Apollo's brow, and over the robust body of Zeus,
I shall strew precious stones and gold and ivory.
My brain moves now like an oriental peacock in my hard,
Aeginan skull.

FIRST GREEK   Let's proceed, dear comrade, toward this gathering. I see
multi-colored tents, people shouting, crying and clapping
their hands in the air;
And a slim, naked ascetic sits cross-legged, with lowered
eyelids, under a dry tree, sunk in an ecstatic,
incomprehensible happiness.

SECOND GREEK   My heart cries out, comrade, that this is the sage we've been
seeking. See how his arms and legs glow, how his robe
shines like a gold cloud at dusk,
How his face moves, serene and suspended, like a spirit.
The small bronze statue of Athena we brought with us as a
holy gift from Greece leaps in my bosom, comrade, as
though it is frightened.

MOGALANA   Don't go any further, don't talk, don't disrupt the holy
gathering.

FIRST AND   We wish to speak with the Buddha.
SECOND GREEK

155

MOGALANA	O human images of distant lands, what country do you call your own?
FIRST GREEK	We are the children of a meager land with azure seashores; we've been walking for months, like two pilgrims, Advancing always toward the rising sun.
MOGALANA	And what, I wonder, are you seeking, fellow-travellers, toward the rising sun?
FIRST GREEK	We've learned that a wise man was born past the Euphrates, that he travels from city to city and puts the thoughts and deeds of men in order, And we've come, that he may give us laws to take back to our country.
MOGALANA	There is no country, there are no laws, there is no wise man, there are no Indies. Nothing exists.
FIRST GREEK	*(To the Second Greek.)* I think, beloved friend, that we've come to the land of the Lotus-Eaters. This dream-taken nobleman has tasted the sweet, poisoned fruit and remembers nothing now; his memory has cleansed and emptied. He sits under a white cypress tree beside the well of Forgetfulness, his whole body is a bottomless jug from which the world pours.
SECOND GREEK	Comrade, let me speak to him, let me hold Greece up before his clouded eyes, that he may be enlightened and his mind awaken. *(To Mogalana.)* I saw a youth in Aegina, when he was returning in his curved ship as a victor from Olympia. He jumped from the ship's prow, rose from the waves, stepped on the hard, foaming shore and walked ahead, gleaming in the sun like a bronze god. The whole island came to the shore to greet him — they tore down the walls of the city that he might pass through. And I — do you hear, ascetic? — I approached him, touched him with this hand, grasped his knees, his thighs, his back, his firm neck, his curly, crowned head... I admired the power, the serenity, the nobility of the human species. I said: The species of man is more handsome

than the horse, more multi-faced than water, richer than
the richest imagination.

There is no greater joy than to have eyes and hands to see
and touch the body of man.

MOGALANA   Shadows! Shadows! Shadows!

FIRST GREEK   O Naked Sophist, those barbarians who trampled Marathon
one morning were not shadows. Our women on the ships
tore their hair, the plain flooded with barbaric tents and
horses, and the sea was thick with red and yellow banners.

And when the triumphal hymn resounded: "Onward young
men of the Hellenes!" our bodies were not shadows, nor
our blood, nor our beating hearts.

That longed for freedom.

MOGALANA   You were fighting shadows with shadows.

Brothers, these are Hellenes, the eternal children of the
imagination, the mindless fish that frisk and play inside
the traps of fishermen, thinking

They are frisking and playing freely in the vast sea.

Their histories are but a dream made up of blue waves, of
meager farms, of ships and horses. With these nonexisting
elements they play, work and create wars, gods, laws and
cities in the drowsy air.

Unfortunate race! For years you fought in Troy for Helen,
and you never suspected you were fighting only for the
shadow of Helen.

You armed ships, you set out together with leaders, prophets,
horses; you travelled in your sleep; you spied a castle made
of clouds, and your blood caught fire; you shouted: "This
is Troy! This is Troy!"

You shaded your eyes with your hand, discerned black spots
moving on the walls, and you shouted, "These are our
enemies!" And the shadows merged, separated, merged
again on the ground

For ten years.

And all this, O unfortunate race, was a game of light and
darkness...The spirit of the Cunning One sat cross-legged
in the air and created the castle, the ships, the sea and
Achilles' wrath and Helen's beauty.

157

FIRST GREEK   And if Helen were a shadow, Naked Sophist, blessed be her
               shadow! For in fighting for that shadow we widened our
               minds, strengthened our bodies and returned to our
               country, our brains filled with wandering and manliness,
               our ships
               Filled with valor, embroidered garments and oriental women.
               For ten years we spilled our blood as Helen's shadow drank,
               and slowly, tenderly wrapped itself in human flesh. And
               after ten years of pleading and fighting, Helen stood before
               us, her pulsing body warm and firm, her wavy hair playing
               in the sea and wind till all the Greeks were blinded by the
               realization of this incomparable woman's beauty; and those
               ten years flared and vanished in our brains like a flash
               of lightning —
               And all the mountaintops of Greece glowed brightly in
               proclaiming the miracle.
               Generations passed and disappeared but immortal Helen lives
               on in song; she sits at the tables of noblemen and in the
               assemblies of the people. She climbs at night into the beds
               of newlyweds like a bride, and all the daughters of Greece
               resemble her; she is the wife of all the Greeks.

SECOND GREEK   Blessed be the gods! This is how we Greeks give flesh to
               shadows, this is how we work and carve the air — as
               though it were marble.
               All the Earth, O ascetic, imagines a Helen plunged in tears
               and tricks, newly-bathed, as her small, bloodied instep
               glows,
               Like the instep of Victory.

MOGALANA   O vain visions of the intoxicated head, O Ephemeral
               Creatures! How long will you flounder like male scorpions
               caught in the erotic deathly teeth of Life — the great female
               Scorpion?
               Wake up, uproot desire, rip out your entrails and shout:
               "I want no more!"
               Smother your hearts and your brains, that they may not
               babble and infect the immortal silence. Listen: the hills
               are shouting, the waters are shouting, tree leaves are
               moving like lips and shouting:
               "Come, come! You'll become one with the earth, with the
               kindly rain and the holy wind; you'll lie down at the

roots of trees in the cool, underground darkness; you'll
pour out again into the earthen womb of the Mother.
Come! Come!"

FIRST GREEK   I will not come! I lean over my heart and hear the whole
Earth calling me: "I am the dark animal; rise, my son,
enlighten me! I am the moment that appears and vanishes;
rise, give me voice, give me body, kiss me, make me
immortal."

Air is good, good and real are water, bread and earth. I open
my eyes, my ears; I see, hear, smell and rejoice in the
upper world. And if this ship of Earth were to sink with all
its crew and cargo, with all its souls —

I, O ascetic, will resist and fight to the death to save it.

Like the brave sailor who works the pump night and day as
his ship takes in water, and the water constantly rises,
certain and unconquerable, one hair's breadth every hour,

While some on the ship cross their hands, others curse, and
others weep or raise their eyes to the heavens —

And only he, stubbornly, biting his lips, raises and lowers his
hands, working the pump incessantly, transforming futility
into bravery,

Thus do I try to work the ship of Earth we have boarded and
that is slowly filling with water.

This is what I like, this is what my heart wants. I listen: All
the mountains, the rivers, the trees, the sea, call to me:
"Give me a face that I may not vanish; look at me that I
may live!"

MOGALANA   Light-headed, Ephemeral Creatures! Never has the cunning
spirit of life cast its fishhook more skillfully.

Rise, throw off the blinders from your eyes and look beyond
at chaos! All things march on toward death; march on with
them. The free man is he who takes the inhuman law of
nature and — easily, willingly — turns it into his own law.

The earth spins for a moment in chaos, its crust opens, it
festers, it fills with plants, animals, people, it fills with
ideas and gods — like a wound filling with worms.

It was Buddha who first saw the onrush of the Universe, he
saw the eternal law and said:

"This onrush is ours; this is the law I enacted; I march on
toward death, a free man."

159

Unfortunate man! You sit at the crossroads of the Cunning
One and the sweat runs from your armpits; women and
men and cities detach themselves from your loins, ships
set out from your sweating breasts and sink in the air...
Rebel! Don't cover the abyss with visions! Raise the gaudy
curtain — the stars and the seas, men and gods; keep chaos
open and look: nothing exists!

FIRST GREEK   Other gods rule us, O ascetic; their nostrils steam, their hearts
beat, they sit at our tables, they snuggle at our hearths,
they climb into our beds,
They couple with our wives, we couple with their goddesses,
and our bloods intermingle. The swarming breed of
mankind is refined, brightened, deified; the race of the gods
is sweetened, warmed and pacified.
Before we came, the immortals shrieked like vultures; they
ranted and could never fasten their minds on simple, sober
words;
But we hunted words high above chaos, we brought them
down to earth, cut their wings and fastened them over the
abyss
Like Wingless Victories.
We raised cyclopean walls around the Mind and would not
allow madness to enter.
Like a coral atoll embedded in the restless bowels of the
Ocean, that with unending struggle works and transforms
currents into stone,
Then opens, spreads, secures itself, heaps carcass upon
carcass, transforming death's trophies into strata of life
that slowly, slowly become an island,
Like such an island, O Lotus-Eater, do we also erect man's
mind above chaos.
We conquered fear by erecting a small, peaceful, armored
statue of Athena before the abyss.
We took a rock, carved a smile on it, and the whole rock of
the world smiled.
And now, as an antidote for the poisoned lotus that crumbles
the foundations of your holy Memory, we bring a gift from
luminous Greece for your leader — this bronze, fully-armed
small statue of Athena. Step back, ascetic, don't get in our
way; we've come to speak with the Buddha.

MOGALANA	O children of the imagination; don't go near the crystal-clear fountain of truth; you'll see your true faces and be frightened. Stand on the outside circle of the arena, with cardinals, hoopoes and peacocks, Then fall to the earth, bow down and worship.
FIRST GREEK	We do not bow down and worship. We will stand erect as we speak with him — that is the custom in Greece. O great sage who bring, we hear, a new measurement to measure truth and falsehood, who bring new laws to separate the just from the unjust, And proclaim new motives for love, listen to our voices. We have come from the navel of earth to this edge of the world to hear your word, to select whatever suits us, to take it with us and to leave. We have cities and laws, we have arenas, theatres, temples and oracles. We have ships and silver-leaved olive trees and grapes and figs; we have all the riches, But we lack one: we lack concord. We fight, brother against brother, and our gods are divided too, and fight like humans. Dissension has risen and seized even the heavens. O Serene Law-giver, all silence and all smiles, open your mouth, give us a new law of love.
PEOPLE	Buddha turns and his almond eyes gaze upon the strangers. He smiles with sweetness and tolerance…The smile of Buddha covers the two odd pilgrims like a setting sun.
FIRST GREEK	O silent sage, you've heard the voice of Greece; why don't you answer?
SECOND GREEK	Quiet, my brother; he has answered; don't you feel it? My heart has overbrimmed with his reply. A deep, serene smile overbrims from the Buddha's brain; it spills over his lips, his chin, his neck… It's not a smile, it's light and it licks the world.
FIRST GREEK	Beloved friend, it seems to me you've tasted of that barbaric fruit, the lotus, and that it has unsettled your mind.
SECOND GREEK:	Ah, if I could only snatch this smile and take it to our country! This, beloved friend, is the answer we have been seeking for years.

161

FIRST GREEK   Comrade, let us go! This air is heavy and filled with demons!

SECOND GREEK   Where can we go, dear friend? This is our country, this is
                our journey's goal, this holy rock, the Buddha,
                And above him I discern a huge temple made of wings and
                air.

FIRST GREEK   Rise comrade, don't fail your lofty lineage. These are the
               barbarians who trample once again on the steady light of
               Greece. Forward, O young men of Greece! Think of our
               triumphal hymn, think of the morning at Salamis!

SECOND GREEK   Ah, if I could preserve his face in Pentelic marble! I see all
                our twelve gods playing on the rippling flesh of his face.
                His whole face is a suspended drop of water, and inside it the
                sky lights up and darkens, the earth lights up and darkens,
                the universe tearfully laughs;
                I have never enjoyed such infinity with a Greek god.

FIRST GREEK   We must leave! See how his barbaric disciples leap, clap their
               hands and begin to dance. Some laugh, others cry, the
               women undress...

PEOPLE   My eyes have clouded. I see a flaming egg burning under the
          Holy Tree, and in its heart, inside the yellow yolk, a drop
          of light glows, like a seed. It's Buddha!
          I see a giant caterpillar eating the Tree of the world; it eats
          forests, descends into cities, crosses thresholds, and without
          anger, without hunger,
          It eats men and gods and stones drowsily.

MOGALANA   Brothers, bare your bodies, bare your souls, throw into
            Buddha's fire
            Your eyes, your ears, your tongues, your nostrils, your
            phalluses and your wombs!
            Shout: "I renounce the mind and the flesh; I renounce virtue
            and sin, joy and pain; I renounce the Yes, I renounce the
            No! I am free!"

FIRST GREEK   Why do they shout? What do they see? Why do these
               barbarians dance? They contaminate the modest face of
               the earth. Beloved friend, let us go!

SECOND GREEK   Don't resist, brother. Let's join the dance too.

162

Silently, without stirring, soberly, the Buddha, overbrimming
with immortal water, pours into these wine jugs of
humanity.

In the same way, comrade, does our own Dionysos, the
fountain of intoxication, stand soberly and pour out his
intoxication.

Give me your hand, comrade, I will let out a cry, that I may
not burst!

MOGALANA Mercy, mercy, the moment has come, Buddha, speak! Pity the
earth and sky, say a good word.

Speak, Lord, that this world may be saved, may vanish, may
become spirit and no longer exist.

Be quiet, brothers, don't stamp your feet, don't beat your
breasts.

Take the animals and birds as examples, see how quietly and
trustingly

They turn their eyes toward Buddha.

PEOPLE Saripoutta approaches, he kisses the two wheels of law on the
soles of Buddha's feet and spreads a lionskin for him under
the Holy Tree that he may lie down.

Mogalana now opens his arms toward Buddha and prays.

MOGALANA Lord, Lord, thoughts sprout and branch out like twisted horns
between your eyebrows, above your forehead, back behind
your ears and the nape of your neck,

Your mind, Lord, is not like the stud ram who mounts
five or ten ewes, then crawls, shriveled up, into the shade,
his eyes and his saliva dripping as he coughs and creaks
like a cracked water-jug.

Instead, your mind is like the great River, Lord, that waters
villages as it descends, turns watermills, increases, swells,
widens,

And runs overjoyed to the sea.

One day I saw the baby river Yangtze gushing from under
huge mountains; I saw it leap from its crib and toddle on,
giggling playfully, like an infant child trampling the pebbles
lightly with its little, soft feet.

Then slowly it rushed out from the ravines, growing,
increasing, as rocks gave way that it might pass. It
descended, and as it rushed down, its disciples, its

163

tributaries, ran from all parts of the earth and poured into
it. The rains fell from the sky and watered it, the snows on
distant mountain-tops melted and fed it,
And down it came, no longer speaking, no longer laughing,
operating noiselessly, accepting the earth and the sky,
transporting the earth and sky forward without delay,
unhurriedly toward the sea.
Thus does your mind work, Buddha!

OLD MAN Buddha has opened his eyes. Buddha has opened his eyes and
is looking at me!
Ah, suddenly my hair falls out; how did a begging-bowl get
into my hands?

A WOMAN Buddha looked at me, too. He nodded to me! My memory
has emptied and cleansed! My heart has emptied and
cleansed!
I raise the palm of my hand,
I see the bones, I see the marrow inside the bones, I see the
worm eating the marrow, and I see Buddha inside the
worm, sitting cross-legged,
Playing with my son between his fingers.
The Earth, the Great Monastery, has filled with yellow monks!

MOGALANA O Lord, O fully awakened Ascetic, now that you are leaving,
speak the richest, most secret, most powerful word of
Liberation —
Buddha, from all your treasures, choose the Great Pearl!

PEOPLE Buddha has fallen into silent thought; his eyebrows are
moving, rising and falling like a balancing scale.
One by one he is weighing his treasures, and he chooses.
He has reached a decision, his lips move; he has weighed well,
he has found the heaviest Pearl.

MOGALANA O Master, trust us with the one great word of Liberation.

BUDDHA Freedom!

FIRST AND Freedom?
SECOND GREEK

PEOPLE Oh, the dry Tree has sprouted blossoms from its roots to its
crown!
The pure, white flowers are falling, falling on the head, the

164

shoulders, the feet of Buddha.

A deep, compassionate smile is licking his face; his arms and legs are glowing!

FIRST AND
SECOND GREEK   Freedom?

SARIPOUTTA   Hold your breath, brother shadows! Buddha is now passing through the first door of nonexistence; he glows from head to heel and all of him rejoices.

His body rejoices to descend and be consumed in earth; his mind rejoices to leap over his head; his mind rejoices because it is vanishing.

PEOPLE   What do you see? My eyes have dimmed.

Ah, his feet hang over chaos! I bend and look into his eyes: We have all vanished, all drowned, brothers, in their still, black waters; the disciples have vanished, the animals have vanished, the birds and the gods;

The pupils of his eyes have emptied and cleansed.

MOGALANA   O Lord, I cannot tame my heart; forgive me, I weep. Do not go, beloved one!

SARIPOUTTA   Mogalana, he's gone, don't try to keep him by holding him; he's gone!

Now he's passing through the second door of nonexistence; his mind no longer rejoices in vanishing, his body no longer rejoices in returning to its country.

He has passed beyond joy and sorrow — he has become enlightened.

The Victor, the great athlete, has returned, he has returned to his country, and the fortress of his flesh has crumbled; quiet, now the fortress of his mind is crumbling too that he may pass.

All of Buddha has become a light, airy dance; every element of his body, every element of his mind rises, is liberated, becomes a dancer,

And in dancing, vanishes.

The third gate of nonexistence, Mogalana, the third gate opens.

MOGALANA   Ah, I can no longer discern his face, I can no longer make out his feet, I can no longer see his hands that glittered on the

165

ground.

SARIPOUTTA His clothes have emptied, Mogalana, don't search in vain.
Part his saffron robe, and you'll find nothing inside, for all
of Buddha has entered into nonexistence.

His voice has not merged with thunder, his breath has not
found refuge in the air, his eyes have not risen to the sun,
his ears have not become seashells; Buddha has left nothing
unliberated of his great body.

He has turned it all into spirit!

The angel of death has come and found nothing to take; the
angel of life has come and found nothing to take; all of
Buddha has been liberated from life and from death —

He has entered into nonexistence.

*(The canary warbles; all the characters stand dazed and
enchanted for a long while and listen.)*

MAGICIAN *(Takes off the yellow mask, then bows to the Old Nobleman.)*

Nobleman, Old Chiang, the performance is over, the
phantasmagoria has come to an end. With the power of
Mind, we have entered into eternity.

My brain played, leaped, danced, flashed sparks, shot out
tongues, rose, descended like fire in the middle of a
crossroad.

My mind knelt cross-legged at the crossroads where the five
shameless night-revelers meet — sight, hearing, taste, smell,
touch — and it said:

"I will make beasts, I will make men and gods, I will arm
insects, I will arm ideas, I will adorn women, I will raise
cities, I will bring Buddha;

I will bring Buddha, and I will comfort mankind."

My mind played and danced; it wants nothing any more; it
rises and says:

"I will make beasts vanish, and men and gods; I will disarm
insects, I will disarm ideas; I will make women rot, I will
sink cities, I will drive Buddha away!

My game has ended; I want nothing more; I'm tired. I blow,
and this multi-colored, holy performance vanishes.

I blow upon you, Mogalana, O restless, erudite, scheming
thought of my head; we have no more need of you," so
the mind says, and casts you off.

"I blow upon you, Brahma, Siva, Vishnu; we'll have no more

166

births or embraces; the wheel has stopped, we don't need
you anymore, go!"
The world has emptied and cleansed, both water and air have
cleansed; only this head still contaminates the abyss; my
mind breaks away like a flame from the wick of my spine.
I blow on myself and I vanish; I think that I blow on myself
and I vanish!
Nobleman, Old Chiang, warriors, peasant men and women,
my sister whores, the performance has ended, the
phantasmagoria has ended; go with my blessings — to
Nothingness!
(Silence. Only the clarinet plays. Slowly the vision fades,
vanishes; the first set returns. The Old Man hugs his
grandson in his arms, paces back and forth triumphantly.)
The performance is over.

OLD MAN   The performance is over; the phantasmagoria has ended!
O erudite mind, gaudy peacock, may you fare well, Hu-Ming,
for you've filled our hearts with felicity.
(The Women who had taken Mei-Ling to the river return.
They hold extinguished candles.)

WOMEN   She didn't speak, she didn't even open her mouth to say
farewell to the world.
She looked down at the waters, searching with longing eyes,
seeking to find her brother.
Suddenly she let out a happy cry, opened her arms and fell
in; she found him!
Ah, the river swallowed her as though she were a stone, a
bucket of rubbish; it did not know, ah, it did not realize
she was our noble lady.

OLD MAN   Why are you shouting? The performance is over, the fantasy
has ended. Why are you crying? For shame! Did you
understand nothing, then? Did the holy yellow storm burst
over your heads in vain? Didn't the silken net of Buddha
wrap itself around your entrails? Courage, friends,
approach, listen to me.
(Traces a circle on the ground with his staff.)
Here, see, in this small arena of the world, let man's virtue
shine, sisters. We cannot save ourselves from death, but we
can save ourselves from fear. Sisters, turn Necessity into

167

freedom.

Greetings, soul of man; greetings fire, that not even a river
can extinguish!

*(Turns to the Ancestors. Raises his grandson high above his
head.)*

Eh, Ancestors, listen to me for the last time: This is my
grandson, there is no other. Save him, if you can.

Eh, hobgoblins, what do you want with swords and spears
and great wings? Save him, that you may be saved.

O Ancestors, I have heard that you are omnipotent; this child
is the only remaining seed; perform the miracle!

*(The seven panoplies slide down from the wall in a heap. The
Old Man stands with open mouth for several moments, then
suddenly lets out a triumphant cry.)*

Freedom! Freedom!

You're right, Buddha, freedom! I've escaped from the
Ancestors!

(Tramples the panoplies with rage.)

PEOPLE   The clan of Chiang has been uprooted!
The world has collapsed!

OLD MAN   The road behind me has emptied. Desolate, utterly desolate is
the road ahead; and I, in the middle, all alone.

O lofty, uninhabited peak, Freedom!

*(Male and female slaves come up from the cellars in a fury
and approach the Old Man.)*

SLAVES   Our turn has come, Old Man; give us the keys! To eat, to
drink, to make up for lost time!

There are no more masters and slaves; the river has arrived—
And everyone, masters and slaves, will become one!

OLD MAN   *(Laughing bitterly.)*

You blockheads! For generations you've allowed the Chiangs
to eat, drink, kiss your women, sit in cool, shaded
terraces in summer, and beside burning hearths in winter,

And now, you unfortunate wretches, you're remembering
much too late to eat and go satiated to Hades.

SLAVES   Better late than never, Old Chiang.

OLD MAN   That's what slaves say. But noblemen say better never than

168

                    late. Here, take the keys!
                    (Throws them the keys.)
                    You are funnels, all of you! Everything enters clean and
                        shining on one end and comes out filth on the other.
                    Koag, Old Koag, why don't you go with them? Are you
                        weeping? Give me an unkind word, Koag, to ease my
                        sadness now that I'm dying.

OLD KOAG   Master...

OLD MAN   Don't give me a kind word, pity me! Ah, for your sake,
                    Old Koag, God should not...if He had any shame, for your
                    sake, Old Koag, He should not
                Have destroyed the world.
                (To the Magician.)
                Is the end finally approaching, Hu-Ming?

MAGICIAN   Here, *The Chronicles of Man* stop, Old Chiang. Now look
                    at our wise Mandarin; he tears pages from his large
                    notebook and makes paper ships to toss into the river.

OLD MAN   Let's prepare!
                (Claps his hands.)
                Koag, eh young, doe-eyed Koag!

BLOSSOMING   Master, he has fallen face down at Buddha's feet and prays.
CHERRY TREE

OLD MAN   Order him to bring me the paints, the perfumes, the great
                    feathers, and to adorn me!
                The blue Emperor is coming, the Yangtze is walking toward
                    my house. Let's greet him as noblemen.
                (The canary warbles as the Old Man listens ecstatically.)
                I pity only you, canary, soul of man, you! What miracle is
                    this? All your bones are filled with song...
                Old Koag, beloved slave and master, do me one more favor,
                    the last one; hang the cage high, high up on the ceiling,
                    that the canary may die last.
                *(A harrowing cry is heard. Blossoming Cherry Tree crumples
                to the ground. Young Koag appears on the first step,
                staggering, blood running down his face. He has blinded
                himself. He extends a begging-bowl, murmuring in a faint
                voice.)*

YOUNG KOAG	My sister...Blossoming Cherry Tree, my sister...
OLD KOAG	My child! Who blinded you, my child?
YOUNG KOAG	Where are you, my sister? Come, you liked my eyes, take them! *(Offers her the begging-bowl.)*
BLOSSOMING CHERRY TREE	My child!
YOUNG KOAG	I blinded myself and saw the light. The middle wall, the futile world, fell, and I saw the true light – the darkness!
OLD MAN	Alas! Every virtue has two heads; the one is all light, the other total darkness. Blossoming Cherry Tree, rise, courage my child; take him inside, that I may not see him. *(The tower shakes. Roar of waters, beasts growling. The people tremble. They huddle together and let out a cry.)* What is it? I seem to hear beasts growling. *(The Three Sentries enter trembling with fear.)*
FIRST SENTRY	Master, beasts from all the plains and forests have gathered in your courtyard!
SECOND SENTRY	The river drove them away, Master, and they came here, trembling, where it's high, to seek refuge.
THIRD SENTRY	Tigers, monkeys, wolves, jackals; and with them, sheep, oxen, camels...All like brothers now, trembling.
OLD MAN	May you be blessed, Yangtze! You've turned ancient enemies into brothers – tigers and sheep now understand – bless you! – that they are brothers.
WHORES	*(Dragging the men with them.)* Come! Come! We're giving good kisses away! We want nothing, nothing, they're free! Good kisses, sweet kisses, we're giving them free! Eh, musicians, strike up the music so we won't hear! *(They try to dance but their knees buckle. They crumple to the ground and begin to wail.)*
OLD MAN	Unfortunate gods, unfortunate men, unfortunate beasts... lumps of dirt!

Hu-Ming, say a word, a simple word the people may hear to
    help them face death.
To face death, Hu-Ming, without shaming themselves.

MAGICIAN   I said the word you ask for, Old Chiang; didn't you hear it?

OLD MAN   What is that word, Hu-Ming? Say it again!

MAGICIAN   Buddha!

OLD MAN   True! True! But I'm not speaking about us; Buddha is a
    rocky, desolate peak, too high
Even for hawks.
I speak of these sluggards, these half-wits, these hags, these
    trollops!
Look at them wallow — some cry, others still eat and are
    hungry, some kiss and are kissed...and others, even more
    disgusting, hide their money in their bosoms...
Hu-Ming, I loathe man, I don't want man any longer,
    Hu-Ming!
Yangtze, savage monk of Buddha, sweep the earth clean!
    Yangtze, streetcleaner of Buddha, sweep up, cleanse the air!
(The tower now shakes with greater vehemence, the stairs
creak.)

OLD KOAG   Master, someone is climbing the stairs.

OLD MAN   It's the great nobleman, Yangtze; open the doors! Light the
    big lanterns!
(Raises his grandson high.)
We're ready; both of us, my grandson and I are ready.
(Men and women let out a cry. Old Koag lights two huge
silken lanterns with paintings of blue dragons on them to the
left and right of the large door. The canary begins to sing
loudly.)
Open the doors! Stand up! Everyone erect, my friends, to
    welcome him,
So he will not say — for shame! — that fear prevents us from
    standing on our feet.
Eh, you lumps of earth, don't you hear, stand erect! Save
    man's honor!
Musicians, strike up the music; not joyfully, not sadly, but
    proudly!
You come too, Hu-Ming; come too, Old Koag, my brother;

come, grandson; let's stand at the threshold to welcome
him…
Koag, open both leaves of the doors wide!
(Raises his eyes to the ceiling, listens to the chirping.)
Farewell, my canary!
(To the Mandarin.)
You come, too, old man.

MANDARIN   No, I will not come; I've work to do, I've taken on a great
task; I've no time: I'm making paper boats out of *The
Chronicles of Man.*
*(Old Koag opens the large door wide to the frightening roar
of the rising river.)*

MAGICIAN   Nobleman, old Chiang, do you hear the roar? Do you know
who it is?

OLD MAN   *(Softly.)*
Quiet! Quiet! Don't let these wretched people hear you.
They can't endure it!

MAGICIAN   *(Softer.)*
Do you finally understand, my Nobleman, who the Yangtze
is?

OLD MAN   Yes: Buddha!
*(The Old Man walks toward the door. The waters are already
beating against the threshold, roaring. The Old Man folds
his arms and bows.)*
Welcome!
(Curtain.)

THE END